Spell it Yourself!

G. T. Hawker

OXFORD
UNIVERSITY PRESS

OXFORD
UNIVERSITY PRESS

Great Clarendon Street, Oxford OX2 6DP

Oxford University Press is a department of the University of Oxford.
It furthers the University's objective of excellence in research, scholarship,
and education by publishing worldwide in

Oxford New York

Auckland Bangkok Buenos Aires Cape Town Chennai
Dar es Salaam Delhi Hong Kong Istanbul Karachi Kolkata
Kuala Lumpur Madrid Melbourne Mexico City Mumbai Nairobi
São Paulo Shanghai Taipei Tokyo Toronto

Oxford is a registered trade mark of Oxford University Press
in the UK and in certain other countries

© G. T. Hawker 1981

First published in paperback 1962
Second edition in paperback 1981
Redesigned impression for paperback 1994
First published in hardback 1992
Redesigned impression for hardback 1995
This paperback edition 2003

British Library cataloguing in Publication Data available

ISBN 0-19-911169-3

10 9 8 7 6 5 4 3 2 1

Printed in Great Britain by Bell & Bain Ltd

Do you have a query about words, their origin, meaning, use, spelling,
pronunciation, or any other aspect of the English language? Visit our
website at www.askoxford.com where you will be able to find answers
to your language queries.

Contents

Instructions

1   Think hard about the word you wish to spell and try to decide with which two letters it starts.

2   Find these two letters in the Index and you will see the number of the page where the word can be found or where you should begin looking for it.

3   Turn to this page and look down the column under these two letters until you find the word you want. Where there are a lot of words which begin with the same two letters, the first three letters of the words are given at the top of the column to help you find the word you want.

It may be necessary to add the word endings shown in *italics* on the right-hand side of the column in order to build up the complete word you want, e.g.

> **rich**   *er, est, ly, ness, es*
> **hair**   *dresser, -dryer, pin, -slide, -style, s*

Here the words **richer, richest, richly, richness** and **riches** may be built up, and also **hairdresser(s), hair-dryer(s), hairpins(s), hair-slide(s), hair-style(s)** and **hairs.**

Where the last letter or letters of a word are in *italics* these must be left off before adding to the other endings, e.g.

> **happ***y*   *ier, iest, ily, iness.*

Here the *y* must be left off before making:

> **happier, happiest, happily, happiness.**

The plurals of most nouns may be formed by adding the letter, or letters, shown in *italics* on the extreme right of the column. A few nouns have their plurals given in full on the right of the column, and you will notice that some nouns have two plurals, either of which may be used, e.g. **cactuses** or **cacti, hoofs** or **hooves, fish** or **fishes.**

All the words with *ed, ing* after them are verbs or may be used as verbs. If you require the word to end in either *ed* or *ing*, remember the following:

(a) **kick** *ed, ing, s* = **kicked   kicking   kicks**

Here *ed* or *ing* or *s* may be added to the verb without changing the word at all.

(b) **stab** *bed, bing, s* = **stabbed   stabbing   stabs**
   stop *ped, ping, s* = **stopped   stopping   stops**

Here you can see that the final consonant (the last letter) of these verbs has to be doubled before adding *ed* or *ing*.

(c) **blame** *d, ∉ing, s* = **blamed   blaming   blames**

Where a verb ends in a letter **e** the *d* or *s* may be added to the word but the **e** must be dropped before adding *ing*. An ∉ is placed before the *ing* to remind you of this.

   There are a few other verbs which change their endings in different ways. You will usually find these endings printed by the side of, above or below, the verb, e.g.

began		**lie**	*d, s*	**carry**	*ing*
begin	*ning, s*	**lying**		**carr** *ied*	*ies*
begun					

Warning: A word which has a star (*) after it has the same sound, or almost the same sound, as another word; but it has a different meaning and spelling, e.g. **knew* new*; their* there*; which* witch*.** The word endings will help you to decide which of these words you want and so will the words in brackets. These are included to guide you; they are not always exact definitions. The words are paired in small print at the bottom of the page. If you find that you have looked up the wrong word you may easily see how the other is spelt and where it may be found in its correct alphabetical place in the book.

ab   ac

ab		ac	
abandon	ed, ing, ment, s	**academ**y	ies
abate	d, ǿing, ment, s	**accelerate**	d, ǿing, s
abbess	es	**accent**	s
abbey	s	**accept*** (receive)	able, ed, ing, s
abbot	s	**accident**	al, ally, s
abduct	ed, ing, ion, s	**accommodate**	d, ǿing, s
abhor red, ring, rence, rent, s		**accommodation**	
abide	d, ǿing, s	**accompany**	ing
ability	ies	**accompan**ied	ies
ablaze		**accomplish**	ed, ing, es
able	r, st, -bodied	**according**	ly
abnormal	ity, ly	**account**	ed, ing, ant, s
aboard		**accumulate**	d, ǿing, s
abolish	ed, ing, es	**accuracy**	
abominable		**accurate**	ly
abominate	d, ǿing, s	**accusation**	s
Aboriginal	s or **Aborigines**	**accuse**	d, ǿing, s
abound	ed, ing, s	**accustom**	ed, ing, s
about		**ache**	d, ǿing, s
above	-board	**achieve**	d, ǿing, ment, s
abreast		**acid**	s
abroad		**acknowledge**	d, ǿing, s
abrupt	ly, ness	**acknowledg(e)ment**	s
abscess	es	**acorn**	s
absence	s	**acquaint**	ed, ing, ance, s
absent	ed, ing, ly, ee, s	**acquire**	d, ǿing, ment, s
absent-minded	ly, ness	**acre**	age, s
absolute	ly	**acrobat**	ic, s
absorb	ed, ing, ent, s	**across**	
abstain	ed, ing, s	**act**	ed, ing, s
absurd	ity, ly	**actor**	s
abundance		**actress**	es
abundant	ly	**action**	s
abuse	d, ǿing, s	**active**	ly
abysmal	ly	**activit**y	ies
abyss	es	**actual**	ly

ǿ Drop **e** before adding *ing*

* accept / except

ad ae af ag

ad	
adapt	able, ed, ing, or, s
add	ed, ing, s
addition	al, s
adder	s
address	ed, ing, es
adequate	ly
adhere	d, ǿing, s
adhesive	s
adjective	s
adjoin	ed, ing, s
adjust	able, ed, ing, ment, s
admirabl e	y
admiral	s
admiration	
admire	d, ǿing, r, s
admission	s
admit	ted, ting, s
admittance	
adopt	ed, ing, ion, s
adorabl e	y
adore	d, ǿing, s
adorn	ed, ing, ment, s
adrift	
adult	s
advance	d, ǿing, ment, s
advantage	s
adventure	d, ǿing, r, s
adventurous	ly, ness
adverb	s
adversar y	ies
advertise	d, ǿing, r, s
advertisement	s
advice	
advisable	
advise	d, ǿing, r, s
advocate	d, ǿing, s

ae	
aerial	s
aerodrome	s
aeronaut	ic, s
aeroplane	s

af	
affair	s
affect	ed, ing, s
affection	s
affectionate	ly, ness
affix	ed, ing, es
afford	ed, ing, s
afloat	
afraid	
after	
afternoon	s
afterwards	

ag	
again	
against	
age	d, less, -group, s
ageing or aging	
agent	s
aggravate	d, ǿing, s
aggressive	ly, ness
aghast	
agile	ly
agilit y	ies
agitate	d, ǿing, s
ago	
agonize	d, ǿing, s
agon y	ies
agree	able, d, ing, ment, s
agricultur e	al
aground	

ǿ Drop **e** before adding *ing*

ai

aid	ed, ing, s
ail* (be ill)	ed, ing, ment, s
aim	ed, ing, less, lessly, s
air*	ed, ing, crew, mail, tight, man, men
air*	gun, field, line, port, way, s
aircraft	-carrier
Airedale	s
air force	s
air y	ier, iest, ily, iness
aisle* (part of a church; gangway)	s

al

alarm	ed, ing, ist, -bell, -clock, s
album	s
alcohol	ism, ic, s
alcove	s
ale* (beer)	s
alert	ed, ing, ly, ness, s
algebra	
alibi	s
alien	s
alight	ed, ing, s
alike	
alive	
all right	
alley	way, s
alligator	s
allot	ted, ting, ment, s
allow	*ed, ing, ance, s
all y	ies
almond	-blossom, -paste, -tree, s
almost	
alone	
along	side
aloud* (loudly)	

alphabet	ical, ically, s
already	
Alsatian	s
also	
altar* (church table)	s
alter* (change)	ed, ing, ation, s
alternate	d, ǿing, ly, s
alternative	ly, s
although	
altitude	s
altogether	
aluminium	
always	

am

amateur	ish, s
amaze	d, ǿing, ment, s
amber	
ambition	s
ambitious	ly, ness
amble	d, ǿing, s
ambulance	man, men, s
ambush	ed, ing, es
amend	ed, ing, ment, s
amiabl e	y
amid or **amidst**	
amiss	
ammunition	
among or **amongst**	
amount	ed, ing, s
amphibian	s or **amphibia**
amphibious	ly
ample	r, st, ness
amplifier	s
amputate	d, ǿing, s
amuse	d, ǿing, ment, s

ǿ Drop **e** before adding *ing*

*	ail	air	aisle	allowed	altar
	ale	heir	isle	aloud	alter

4

an　　　ap

an	
anaesthetic	*s*
ancestor	*s*
ancestr *y*	*ies*
anchor	*ed, ing, age, s*
ancient	*ly, ness, s*
anemone	*s*
angel	*s*
anger	*ed, ing, s*
angr *y*	*ier, iest, ily*
angle	*d, ȼing, r, s*
anguish	*ed, ing, es*
animal	*s*
ankle	*s*
anniversar *y*	*ies*
announce	*d, ȼing, r, ment, s*
annoy	*ed, ing, ance, s*
annual	*ly, s*
anoint	*ed, ing, ment, s*
anonymous	*ly*
anorak	*s*
another	
answer	*ed, ing, s*
ant	*-eater, -hill, s*
antarctic	
antelope	*s*
antic	*s*
anticipate	*d, ȼing, s*
anticipation	*s*
antique	*-dealer, -shop, s*
antirrhinum	*s*
antiseptic	*s*
antler	*s*
anvil	*s*
anxiet *y*	*ies*
anxious	*ly*
any	*body, one, how, thing, way, where*

ap	
apart	
apartment	*s*
ape	*d, ȼing, s*
apiar *y*	*ies*
apiece	
apologetic	*al, ally*
apologize	*d, ȼing, s*
apolog *y*	*ies*
apostle	*s*
appal	*led, ling, lingly, s*
apparatus	*es* or **apparatus**
apparent	*ly*
appeal	*ed, ing, ingly, s*
appear	*ed, ing, ance, s*
appendicitis	
appetite	*s*
appetizing	*ly*
applaud	*ed, ing, s*
applause	
apple	*-core, -pie, -sauce, -tart, -tree, s*
appliance	*s*
applicant	*s*
application	*s*
apply	*ing*
appl *ied*	*ies*
appoint	*ed, ing, ment, s*
appreciate	*d, ȼing, s*
appreciation	
apprentice	*d, ȼing, ship, s*
approach	*ed, ing, es*
approval	
approve	*d, ȼing, s*
approximate	*ly, d, ȼing, s*
apricot	*s*
April	*-fool, s*
apron	*s*

ȼ Drop **e** before adding *ing*

aq ar   as

aq	
aquarium	s or **aquaria**
aquatic	s
aqueduct	s

ar	
arable	
arc* (curve)	-lamp, -light, s
arcade	s
arch	ed, ing, es
archway	s
archaeological	ly
archaeologist	s
archaeology	
archer	y, s
architect	ure, ural, s
arctic	
are	
aren't (are not)	
area	s
arena	s
argue	d, ǿing, s
argument	ative, s
arise	n, ǿing, s
arithmetic	al
ark* (boat; box)	s
arm	ed, ing, band, chair, ful, hole, pit, s
armada	s
armament	s
armistice	s
armour	ed, y, -plated, -plating
arm y	ies
arose	
around	
arouse	d, ǿing, s
arrange	d, ǿing, r, ment, s

as	
array	ed, ing, s
arrest	ed, ing, s
arrival	s
arrive	d, ǿing, s
arrow	-head, s
arsenic	
art	work, s
artist	ic, ically, s
artful	ly, ness
arter y	ies
article	s
artificial	ity, ly, ness
artillery	man, men

as	
ascend	ed, ing, s
ascent	s
ascertain	ed, ing, s
ash	en, y, es
ashamed	
ashore	
aside	
ask	ed, ing, s
asleep	
asparagus	
asphyxiate	d, ǿing, s
aspirin	s
ass	es
assail	ed, ing, ant, s
assassin	ation, s
assassinate	d, ǿing, s
assault	ed, ing, s
assemble	d, ǿing, s
assembl y	ies
assist	ed, ing, ance, s
assistant	s

ǿ Drop **e** before adding *ing*

* arc
  ark

at

associate	d, ∉ing, s
association	s
assort	ed, ing, ment, s
assume	d, ∉ing, s
assure	d, ∉ing, s
aster	s
asthma	tic, tical
astonish	ed, ing, es, ment
astound	ed, ing, s
astray	
astride	
astrologer	s
astrolog y	ical
astronaut	s
astronomer	s
astronom y	ical
asylum	s

at

ate* (eat)	
athlete	s
athletic	ally, s
Atlantic	
atlas	es
atmosphere	s
atom	ic, -bomb, s
atrocious	ly, ness
attach	ed, ing, able, es
attachment	s
attack	ed, ing, er, s
attain	ed, ing, able, ment, s
attempt	ed, ing, s
attend	ed, ing, ance, s
attendant	s
attention	s
attentive	ly, ness

au   av

attic	s
attitude	s
attract	ed, ing, ion, s
attractive	ly, ness
attribute	d, ∉ing, s

au

auburn	
auction	ed, ing, eer, s
audible	
audience	s
audition	ed, ing, s
August	s
aunt	s
auntie s or **aunt** y	ies
author	s
authoress	es
authorit y	ies
authorize	d, ∉ing, s
autobiograph y	ical, ies
autograph	ed, ing, s
automatic	ally
automation	
autumn	al, s

av

available	
avalanche	s
avenge	d, ∉ing, r, s
avenue	s
average	d, ∉ing, s
aviar y	ies
aviation	
aviator	s
avoid	ed, ing, able, ance, s

∉ Drop **e** before adding *ing*

*   ate
    eight (8)

aw   ax   ba

aw

await	ed, ing, s
awake	d, ∉ing, s
awaken	ed, ing, s
award	ed, ing, s
aware	ness
away	
awe	some, struck, stricken
awful	ly, ness
awhile	
awkward	ly, ness
awning	s
awoke or **awaked**	
awry	

ax

axe	d, ∉ing, -blade, -handle, s
ax is	es
axle	s

ba

babe	s
baboon	s
bab y	ies
bachelor	s
back	ed, ing, cloth, ground, yard, s
backward	ly, ness, s
bacon	
bad	-tempered, ly, ness
badge	s
badger	ed, ing, s
badminton	-racket
baffle	d, ∉ing, s
bag	ged, ging, ful, -snatcher, s
baggage	
bagg y	ier, iest, ily, iness
bagpipe	s
bail* (wicket cross-piece)	s
bait	ed, ing, s
bake	d, ∉ing, r, house, s
baker y	ies
balance	d, ∉ing, r, s
balcon y	ies
bald	ing, er, est, ly, ness, -headed
bale* (bundle)	d, ∉ing, r, s
bale* { out of plane or	d, ∉ing, r, s
bail* { throw out water }	ed, ing, er, s
ball*	-game, point, -pen, room, s
ballast	
ballerina	s
ballet	-dancing, -dancer, -shoe, s
balloon	ed, ing, ist, s
ballot	ed, ing, -paper, s
bamboo	s
ban	ned, ning, s
banana	s
band	ed, ing, sman, smen, stand, s
bandage	d, ∉ing, s
bandit	s
bang	ed, ing, er, s
bangle	s
banish	ed, ing, es, ment
banister	s
banjo	es or s
bank	ed, ing, er, -book, note, s
bankrupt	ed, ing, s, cy
banner	s
banquet	ed, ing, s
bantam	s
baptism	s
baptize	d, ∉ing, s
bar	red, ring, maid, s

∉ Drop **e** before adding *ing*

*   bail   ball
    bale   bawl

barbecue	d, ǿing, s
barbed	-wire
barber	s
bare* (naked; empty)	ly, ness, d, ǿing, s
bargain	ed, ing, er, s
barge	d, ǿing, e, -pole, s
bark	ed, ing, er, s
barley	corn, -sugar, -water, s
barn	-dance, -owl, yard, s
barnacle	s
barometer	s
baron* (lord)	et, s
barrack	ed, ing, er, -room, -square, s
barrel	ful, s
barren* (bare; empty)	ly, ness
barricade	d, ǿing, s
barrier	s
barrister	s
barrow	-boy, s
barter	ed, ing, er, s
base	d, ǿing, r, st, ly, less, ness, -line, s
baseball	s
basement	s
bash	ed, ing, es
bashful	ly, ness
basin	ful, s
bask	ed, ing, s
basket	ball, ful, s
bat	ted, ting, sman, smen, s
batch	es
bath	ed, ing, mat, robe, room, -water, s
bathe	d, ǿing, r, s
bathing-costume	s
baton	s
battalion	s
batter	ed, ing, s
batter y	ies

battle	d, ǿing, axe, field, ship, s
bawl* (shout; cry out)	ed, ing, s
bay	-window, s
bayonet	ed, ing, s
bazaar	s

be

beach* (seashore)	ed, ing, es
beacon	s
bead	ed, ing, work, s
beak	s
beaker	s
beam	ed, ing, s
bean* (plant)	-bag, pole, stalk, s
bear* (carry; endure)	able, ing, er, s
bear* (animal)	skin, s
beard	ed, s
beast	s
beastl y	ier, iest, iness
beat* (hit; defeat)	en, ing, er, s
beautiful	ly
beaut y	ies
beaver	s
became	
because	
beckon	ed, ing, s
become	ǿing, s
bed	ded, ding, clothes, side, time, room, s
bee	hive, line, keeper, s
beech* (tree)	es
beef	burger, eater, steak, s
been* (past of be)	
beer	y, -barrel, -bottle, -can, s
beet* (vegetable)	root, s
beetle	s
before	hand

ǿ Drop e before adding *ing*

* bare	baron	bawl	beach	bean	beat
bear	barren	ball	beech	been	beet

bi

beg	ged, ging, s
beggar	ly, s
began	
begin	ning, ner, s
begun	
begone	
behave	d, ∉ing, s
behaviour	
behead	ed, ing, s
behind	hand
being	s
belief	s
believe	d, ∉ing, r, s
bell	-ringer, -tent, -tower, s
bellow	ed, ing, er, s
belong	ed, ing, s
below	
belt	ed, ing, s
bench	es
bend	ing, er, s
bent	
beneath	
benefit	ed, ing, s
benevolent	ly
beret* (cap)	s
berry* (fruit)	ies
berth* (bunk; moor a ship)	ed, ing, s
beside	s
besiege	d, ∉ing, r, s
best	-seller
bet	ted, ting, ter, s
betray	al, ed, ing, er, s
better	ed, ing, s
between	
beware	
bewilder	ed, ing, ment, s
beyond	

bi

Bible	s
bicker	ed, ing, s
bicycle	d, ∉ing, -clip, -pump, s
bid	ding, der, s
bide	d, ∉ing, s
big	ger, gest, ness
bike	d, ∉ing, s
bikini	s
bilberr y	ies
bilge	-water, -pump, s
bilious	ly, ness
bill	ed, ing, s
billet	ed, ing, s
billiard	-ball, -cue, -room, -table, s
billion	s
billow	ed, ing, s
bind	ing, er, s
bingo	-hall, s
binoculars	
biograph y	ical, ies
biolog y	ical, ist
biped	s
birch	es
bird	-bath, -cage, -seed, -table, s
birth* (born)	day, mark, place, rate, s
biscuit	s
bisect	ed, ing, ion, s
bishop	s
bison	**bison**
bit	ty, s
bitch	es
bite	∉ing, r, s
bitten	
bitter	er, est, ly, ness
bittern	s
bivouac	ked, king, s

∉ Drop **e** before adding *ing*

*	beret	berth
	berry	birth
	bury	

bl   bo

bl

black	*ed, ing, er, est, ness, smith, s*
black	*-beetle, bird, board, -currant, s*
blackberry	*ing*
blackberr *ied*	*ies*
blacken	*ed, ing, s*
blackmail	*ed, ing, er, s*
blade	*d, s*
blame	*d, ∅ing, less, s*
blancmange	*s*
blank	*ed, ing, er, est, ly, ness, s*
blanket	*s*
blare	*d, ∅ing, s*
blast	*ed, ing, s*
blaze	*d, ∅ing, s*
blazer	*s*
bleach	*ed, ing, es*
bleak	*er, est, ly, ness*
bleat	*ed, ing, s*
bleed	*ing, s*
bled	
blend	*ed, ing, er, s*
bless	*ed, ing, ings, es*
blew* (blow)	
blind	*ed, ing, er, est, ly, ness, s*
blindfold	*ed, ing, s*
blind-man's-buff	
blink	*ed, ing, er, s*
blister	*ed, ing, s*
blizzard	*s*
block	*age, ed, ing, s*
blockade	*d, ∅ing, s*
blond (masc.)	*er, est, s*
blonde (fem.)	*r, st, s*
blood	*hound, shed, -stained, thirsty, y*
bloom	*ed, ing, s*
blossom	*ed, ing, s*

blot	*ted, ting, ter, s*
blouse	*s*
blow	*n, ing, y, er, lamp, pipe, s*
blue* (colour)	*r, st, ness, bell, bottle, s*
blunder	*ed, ing, s*
blunt	*ed, ing, er, est, ly, ness, s*
blush	*ed, ing, es*
bluster	*ed, ing, y, s*

bo

boar* (male pig)	*s*
board* (wood; ship; lodge)	*ed, ing, s*
boarder* (one who boards; lodger)	*s*
boast	*ed, ing, er, s*
boastful	*ly, ness*
boat	*ed, ing, er, man, men, -race, s*
bob	*bed, bing, -sleigh, s*
bod *y*	*ies*
bog	*ged, ging, s*
bogg *y*	*ier, iest, iness*
boil	*ed, ing, er, s*
boisterous	*ly, ness*
bold	*er,* est, ly, ness*
bolt	*ed, ing, s*
bomb	*ed, ing, er, -proof, shell, sight, s*
bombard	*ed, ing, ment, s*
bone	*d, ∅ing, ∅y, -dry, -idle, -shaker, s*
bonfire	*s*
bonnet	*s*
bonn *y*	*ier, iest, ily, iness*
book	*ed, ing, case, let, seller, stall, s*
booking office	*s*
boom	*ed, ing, s*
boot	*ed, ing, lace, s*
border* (edge)	*ed, ing, er, less, line, s*
bore* (drill hole; weary)	*d,* ∅ing, dom, s*

*∅ Drop **e** before adding ing*

*	blew	boar	board	boarder	bolder
	blue	bore	bored	border	boulder

born* (birth)	
borne* (carried)	
borrow	ed, ing, er, s
boss	ed, ing, es
boss y	ier, iest, ily, iness
botan y	ical, ist
both	
bother	ed, ing, some, s
bottle	d, ∉ing, -opener, s
bottom	ed, ing, less, s
bough* (branch)	s
bought (buy)	
boulder* (large rock)	s
bounce	d, ∉ing, r, s
bound	ed, ing, less, s
boundar y	ies
bouquet	s
bow* (bend)	ed, ing, s
bow	man, men, shot, string, -tie, s
bowl	ed, ing, er, s
bowl	ful, s
box	ed, ing, es
boxer	s
Boxing Day	s
boy* (lad)	ish, hood, -friend, s
Boy Scout	s

br

brace	d, ∉ing, s
bracelet	s
bracken	
bracket	ed, ing, s
brag	ged, ging, gart, s
braid	ed, ing, s
brain	ed, ing, less, storm, wave, s
brain y	ier, iest, ily, iness

brake* (to stop)	d, ∉ing, s
bramble	s
branch	ed, ing, es
brand	ed, ing, -new, s
brandish	ed, ing, es
brand y	ies
brass	es
brave	d, ∉ing, r, st, ly, s
bravery	
bravo	s
brawl	ed, ing, er, s
brawn	
brawn y	ier, iest, iness
brazen	ed, ing, ly, ness
brazier	s
bread*	-bin, -board, -sauce, -crumb, s
breadth	s
break*	able, age, ing, er, -down, water, s
breakfast	ed, ing, -table, -room, s
breast	ed, ing, plate, -stroke, s
breath	less, lessly, -taking, s
breathe	d, ∉ing, r, s
bred* (brought-up)	
breed	ing, er, s
breeze	s
breez y	ier, iest, ily, iness
brew	ed, ing, er, s
brewer y	ies
bribe	d, ∉ing, ry, s
brick	ed, ing, laying, layer, work, yard, s
bridal* (of a bride, wedding)	-gown
bride	groom, smaid, s
bridge	d, ∉ing, head, s
bridle* (horse's headgear)	-path, road, s
brief	ed, ing, er, est, ly, ness, case, s
brigade	s
brigand	s

∉ Drop **e** before adding *ing*

bright	*er, est, ly, ness*
brighten	*ed, ing, s*
brilliance	
brilliant	*ly*
brim	*med, ming, ful, s*
bring	*ing, s*
brink	*s*
brisk	*er, est, ly, ness*
bristle	*d, ¢ing, s*
bristly	*ier, iest, iness*
brittle	*ness*
broad	*er, est, ly, -minded, side, s*
broaden	*ed, ing, s*
broadcast	*ing, er, s*
brocade	*s*
broccoli	
broke	
broken	*-down, -hearted*
bronchitis	
bronze	*d, ¢ing, s*
brooch	*es*
brood	*ed, ing, y, s*
brook	*s*
broom	*stick, s*
broth	*s*
brother	*ly, s*
brother(*s*)**-in-law**	
brought (bring)	
brow	*s*
brown	*ed, ing, er, est, ish, ness, s*
brownie	*s*
bruise	*d, ¢ing, r, s*
brunette	*s*
brush	*ed, ing, es*
Brussels sprouts	
brutal	*ity, ly*
brute	*s*

bu

bubble	*d, ¢ing, -bath, -gum, s*
bubbly	*ier, iest, iness*
buccaneer	*s*
buck	*ed, ing, skin, s*
bucket	*ful, s*
buckle	*d, ¢ing, s*
bud	*ded, ding, s*
budge	*d, ¢ing, s*
budgerigar	*s*
budget	*ed, ing, s*
buffalo	*es* or **buffalo**
buffer	*s*
buffet	*ed, ing, s*
bugle	*-call, r, s*
build	*ing, er, s*
built	
bulb	*s*
bulge	*d, ¢ing, s*
bulk	
bulky	*ier, iest, ily, iness*
bull	*dog, fight, frog, ring, -terrier, s*
bull's-eye	*s*
bulldoze	*d, ¢ing, r, s*
bullet	*-hole, -proof, -wound, s*
bulletin	*s*
bullion	
bullock	*s*
bully	*ing*
bullied	*ies*
bulrush	*es*
bumble-bee	*s*
bump	*ed, ing, er, s*
bumpy	*ier, iest, ily, iness*
bunch	*ed, ing, es*
bundle	*d, ¢ing, s*
bung	*ed, ing, -hole, s*

¢ Drop ¢ before adding *ing*

bungalow	s
bungle	d, øing, r, s
bunk	s
bunker	ed, ing, s
Bunsen burner	s
bunting	
buoy* (floating marker)	ant, ed, ing, s
burden	ed, ing, some, s
bureau	x or s
burglar	-alarm, s
burglar y	ies
burgle	d, øing, s
burial	-ground, -place, s
burl y	ier, iest, ily, iness
burn	ed, ing, er, s
burnt or **burned**	
burrow	ed, ing, er, s
burst	ing, s
bury* (cover)	ing
bur ied	ies
bus	man, men, es
busb y	ies
bush	es
bush y	ier, iest, ily, iness
business	man, men, es
bustle	d, øing, r, s
busy	ing, ness
bus ied	ier, iest, ily, ies
butcher	ed, ing, s
butler	s
butter	ed, ing, scotch, cup, s
butterfl y	ies
button	ed, ing, -hole, s
buy* (purchase)	ing, er, s
buzz	ed, ing, es
buzzer	s
buzzard	s

by

by* (near to, etc.)	
bye* (a run)	s
bygone	s
by-pass	ed, ing, es
bystander	s
byway	s

ca

cabaret	s
cabbage	s
cabin	-boy, s
cabinet	-maker, s
cable	d, øing, gram, -car, s
cackle	d, øing, r, s
cactus	es or **cacti**
caddie* (golfer's club-carrier)	d, s
caddying	
cadd y* (tea box)	ies
cadet	s
cadge	d, øing, r, s
café	s
cafeteria	s
cage	d, øing, s
cake	d, øing, s
calamit y	ies
calculate	d, øing, s
calculation	s
calculator	s
calendar	s
calf	skin, **calves**
call	ed, ing, er, s
calm	ed, ing, er, est, ly, ness, s
came	
camel	-hair, s
camera	man, men, s
camouflage	d, øing, s

é Drop e before adding ing

*	buoy	bury		buy	caddie
	boy	beret		bye	caddy
		berry		by	

camp	*ed, ing, er, -bed, -fire, site, s*	**career**	*ed, ing, s*
campaign	*ed, ing, er, s*	**caress**	*ed, ing, es*
canal	*s*	**cargo**	*es*
canar *y*	*ies*	**caricature**	*d, ǿing, s*
cancel	*led, ling, lation, s*	**carnation**	*s*
candidate	*s*	**carnival**	*s*
candle	*-light, wick, stick, s*	**carnivorous**	
cand *y*	*ied, ies*	**carol**	*led, ling, ler, -singer, s*
cane	*d, ǿing, s*	**carpenter**	*s*
cannibal	*ism, s*	**carpentry**	
cannon	*ed, -ball, -shot, s* or **cannon**	**carpet**	*ed, ing, -sweeper, s*
cannot		**carriage**	*way, s*
can't (cannot)		**carrot**	*s*
canoe	*d, ing, ist, s*	**carry**	*ing*
canteen	*s*	**carr** *ied*	*ies*
canter	*ed, ing, s*	**carrier**	*-bag, -pigeon, s*
canvas* (strong cloth)	*es*	**cart**	*ed, ing, -load, -horse, -wheel, s*
canvass* (seek votes, orders)	*ed, ing, es*	**carton**	*s*
canyon	*s*	**cartoon**	*ed, ing, ist, s*
capabl *e*	*y*	**cartridge**	*-belt, -case, s*
cape	*s*	**carve**	*d, ǿing, r, s*
capital	*s*	**cascade**	*d, ǿing, s*
capsize	*d, ǿing, s*	**case**	*s*
capsule	*s*	**cash**	*ed, ing, -box, es*
captain	*ed, ing, s*	**cashier**	*s*
captive	*s*	**cask**	*s*
captivit *y*	*ies*	**casket**	*s*
capture	*d, ǿing, s*	**casserole**	*d, ǿing, s*
car	*-load, -park, port, s*	**cassette**	*-player, -recorder, s*
caramel	*s*	**cast**	*ing, s*
caravan	*ned, ning, ner, s*	**castaway**	*s*
carcass *es* or **carcase**	*s*	**castle**	*s*
card	*board, -game, -room, -table, s*	**castor oil**	
cardigan	*s*	**casual**	*ly, ness, s*
care	*d, ǿing, free, taker, s*	**casualt** *y*	*ies*
careful	*ly, ness*	**catalogue**	*d, ǿing, s*
careless	*ly, ness*	**catapult**	*ed, ing, s*

ǿ Drop **e** before adding *ing*

*   canvas
    canvass

ce   ch_a

catastrophe	*s*	cemeter *y*	*ies*
catch	*ing, es*	cent* (coin)	*s*
catch *y*	*ier, iest, iness*	centigrade	
cater	*ed, ing, er, s*	centimetre	*s*
caterpillar	*s*	central	*ly*
cathedral	*s*	centre	*d, ẹing, -forward, -piece, s*
Catherine wheel	*s*	centur *y*	*ies*
Catholic	*s*	cereal* (wheat, oats, etc.)	*s*
catkin	*s*	ceremon *y*	*ies*
cattle	*-market, -shed, -show, -truck*	certain	*ly, ty*
caught		certificate	*s*
cauldron	*s*		
cauliflower	*s*		

ch

cause	*d, ẹing, s*
caution	*ed, ing, s*
cautious	*ly, ness*
cavalier	*s*
cavalry	
cave	*d, ẹing, -man, -men, -dweller, s*
cavern	*s*
cavit *y*	*ies*

chaffinch *es*
chain *ed, ing, -mail, -saw, -store, s*
chair *ed, ing, man, woman, -lift, s*
chalet *s*
chalk *ed, ing, s*
chalk *y* *ier, iest, iness*
challenge *d, ẹing, r, s*
chamber *maid, s*
chamois *-leather*
champagne *s*
champion *ed, ing, ship, s*

ce

cease	*d, ẹing, less, lessly, s*
cedar	*s*
ceiling* (roof of room)	*s*
celandine	*s*
celebrate	*d, ẹing, s*
celebration	*s*
celebrit *y*	*ies*
celery	
cell* (small room)	*s*
cellar* (underground room)	*s*
cello	*s*
cellophane	
cement	*ed, ing, -mixer, s*

chance *d, ẹing, s*
chandelier *s*
change *able, d, ẹing, s*
channel *led, ling, s*
chant *ed, ing, s*
chaos
chaotic *ally*
chapel *s*
chapter *s*
char *red, ring, woman, women, s*
character *istic, s*
charade *s*

ẹ Drop **e** before adding *ing*

charcoal		**chick**	*weed, s*	
charge	*d, øing, r, s*	**chicken**	*-feed, -wire, s* or **chicken**	
chariot	*eer, s*	**chicken-pox**		
charit *y*	*ies*	**chief**	*ly, tain, s*	
charm	*ed, ing, er, s*	**chilblain**	*s*	
chart	*ed, ing, room, s*	**child**	*ish, hood, like, less,* **children**	
charter	*ed, ing, s*	**chill**	*ed, ing, er, s*	
chase	*d, øing, r, s*	**chill** *y*	*ier, iest, ily, iness*	
chasm	*s*	**chime**	*d, øing, s*	
chat	*ted, ting, s*	**chimney**	*-pot. -stack, -sweep, s*	
chatter	*ed, ing, er, s*	**chimpanzee**	*s*	
chatt *y*	*ier, iest, ily, iness*	**chin**	*-strap, s*	
chauffeur	*s*	**china**	*-shop, ware*	
cheap	*er, est, ly, ness*	**chink**	*ed, ing, s*	
cheapen	*ed, ing, s*	**chintz**	*es*	
cheat	*ed, ing, er, s*	**chip**	*ped, ping, per, s*	
check*	*ed, ing, er, -list, -out, -point, s*	**chirp**	*ed, ing, s*	
check* (pattern)	*ed, s*	**chirp** *y*	*ier, iest, ily, iness*	
cheek	*ed, ing, -bone, s*	**chisel**	*led, ling, s*	
cheek *y*	*ier, iest, ily, iness*	**chivalrous**	*ly*	
cheer	*ed, ing, -leader, s*	**chivalry**		
cheerful	*ly, ness*	**chlorine**		
cheerless	*ly, ness*	**chloroform**	*ed, ing, s*	
cheer *y*	*ier, iest, ily, iness*	**chocolate**	*s*	
cheese	*burger, cake, cloth, -straw, s*	**choice**	*r, st, ly, ness, s*	
chef	*s*	**choir*** (of singers)	*-boy, -master, s*	
chemical	*ly, s*	**choke**	*d, øing, s*	
chemist	*s*	**choose**	*øing, s*	
chemistry		**chose**	*n*	
cheque* (money-order)	*-book, s*	**chop**	*ped, ping, per, s*	
cherish	*ed, ing, es*	**chopstick**	*s*	
cherr *y*	*ies*	**chorus**	*ed, ing, es*	
chess	*-board, -piece, -man, -men*	**chow**	*s*	
chest	*s*	**christen**	*ed, ing, s*	
chestnut	*-tree, s*	**Christ**		
chew	*ed, ing, y, er, s*	**Christian**	*ity, s*	
chewing-gum		**Christmas**	*-box, es, -time, -tree, sy*	

ø Drop **e** before adding *ing*

*   check   choir
        cheque   quire

chromium	-plated, -plating
chrysalis	es
chrysanthemum	s
chubby	ier, iest, ily, iness
chuckle	d, ǿing, s
chug	ged, ging, s
chum	med, ming, s
chummy	ier, iest, ily, iness
chunk	s
church	es
churchyard	s
churn	ed, ing, s
chute* (a slide)	s
chutney	s

ci

cider or **cyder**	s
cigar	-case, -holder, -lighter, s
cigarette	-case, -holder, -lighter, s
cinder	-path, -track, s
cine-	camera, film, projector
cinema	-goer, s
circle	d, ǿing, s
circular	s
circulate	d, ǿing, s
circulation	s
circumference	s
circumstance	s
circus	es
cistern	s
citizen	s
city	ies
civil	ity, ly
civilian	s
civilization	s
civilize	d, ǿing, s

cl

claim	ed, ing, s
clamber	ed, ing, s
clammy	ier, iest, ily, iness
clamp	ed, ing, s
clang	ed, ing, s
clank	ed, ing, s
clap	ped, ping, per, s
clash	ed, ing, es
clasp	ed, ing, s
class	ed, ing, es, rooms
classic	al, s
clatter	ed, ing, s
claw	ed, ing, s
clay	ey, -pigeon, -pipe, -pit, s
clean	ed, ing, er, est, ly, ness, s
cleanliness	
cleanse	d, ǿing, r, s
clear	ed, ing, er, est, ly, ness, s
clench	ed, ing, es
clergy	man, men
clerk	s
clever	er, est, ly, ness
click	ed, ing, s
client	s
cliff	-top, s
climate	s
climb	ed, ing, er, s
cling	ing, s
clinic	al, ally, s
clink	ed, ing, er, s
clip	ped, ping, per, s
cloak	ed, ing, room, s
clock	ed, ing, wise, work, -tower, s
cloister	ed, ing, s
close (shut)	d, ǿing, s
close (near; stuffy)	r, st, ly, ness

*ǿ Drop **e** before adding ing*

* chute
   shoot

cloth s	**code** d, øing, s
clothe d, øing, s	**coffee** -bar, -bean, -cup, -pot, -table, s
clothes -basket, -horse, -line, -peg	**coffin** s
cloud ed, ing, less, lessly, burst, s	**coil** ed, ing, s
cloudy ier, iest, ily, iness	**coin** age, ed, ing, s
clover s	**coincide** d, øing, s
clown ed, ing, s	**coincidence** s
club bed, bing, house, room, s	**cold** er, est, ish, ly, ness, -storage, s
cluck ed, ing, s	**collapse** d, øing, s
clue less, s	**collapsible**
clump ed, ing, s	**collar** -bone, -stud, s
clumsy ier, iest, ily, iness	**collect** ed, ing, ion, or, s
clung	**college** s
cluster ed, ing, s	**collide** d, øing, s
clutch ed, ing, es	**collision** s
clutter ed, ing, s	**collie** s
	collier s
	colliery ies
co	**colonel***(officer) s
coach man, men, ed, ing, es	**colonize** d, øing, s
coal man, men, -mine, -miner, s	**colon**y ies
coarse*(rough) r, st, ly, ness	**colossal** ly
coast al, ed, ing, line, guard, s	**colour** ed, ing, ful, less, -scheme, s
coat ed, ing, -hanger, s	**column** s
coax ed, ing, es	**comb** ed, ing, s
cobble d, øing, r, -stone, s	**combat** ed, ing, s
cobra s	**combination** s
cobweb by, s	**combine** d, øing, -harvester, s
cock ed, ing, -fight, pit, tail, s	**come** øing, s
cockatoo s	**comedian** (masc.) s
cockerel s	**comedienne** (fem.) s
cockle -shell, s	**comed**y ies
cockney s	**comet** s
cockroach es	**comfort** able, ably, ed, ing, s
cocoa	**comic** al, ally, s
coconut -matting, -milk, -palm, s	**command** ed, ing, er, ment, s
cocoon s	**commemorate** d, øing, s

ø Drop e before adding *ing*

*	coarse	colonel
	course	kernel

con

commence	*d, ǿing, ment, s*	**conceal**	*ed, ing, ment, s*
comment	*ed, ing, ator, s*	**conceit**	*ed, edly*
commentary	*ies*	**concentrate**	*d, ǿing, s*
commerce		**concentration**	
commercial	*s*	**concern**	*ed, ing, s*
commission	*ed, ing, aire, er, s*	**concert**	*s*
commit	*ted, ting, ment, s*	**conclude**	*d, ǿing, s*
committee	*-room, s*	**conclusion**	*s*
common	*er, est, ly, ness, -room, s*	**concrete**	*d, ǿing, s*
commotion	*s*	**condemn**	*ed, ing, ation, s*
communicate	*d, ǿing, s*	**condition**	*ed, ing, er, s*
communication	*s*	**conduct**	*ed, ing, or, s*
communion		**conductress**	*es*
community	*ies*	**conference**	*s*
compact	*s*	**confess**	*ed, ing, es*
companion	*ship, s*	**confession**	*s*
company	*ies*	**confetti**	
comparative	*ly, s*	**confide**	*d, ǿing, s*
compare	*d, ǿing, s*	**confidence**	
comparison	*s*	**confident**	*ial, ially, ly*
compartment	*s*	**confirm**	*ed, ing, ation, s*
compass	*es*	**confiscate**	*d, ǿing, s*
compel	*led, ling, s*	**confuse**	*d, ǿing, s*
compete	*d, ǿing, s*	**confusion**	*s*
competition	*s*	**congratulate**	*d, ǿing, s*
competitor	*s*	**congratulation**	*s*
complain	*ed, ing, s*	**congregate**	*d, ǿing, s*
complaint	*s*	**congregation**	*s*
complete	*d, ǿing, ly, ness, s*	**conjure**	*d, ǿing, s*
complexion	*s*	**conjurer** or **conjuror**	*s*
complicate	*d, ǿing, s*	**conker*** (horse-chestnut)	*s*
compliment	*ed, ing, ary, s*	**connect**	*ed, ing, ion, s*
compose	*d, ǿing, r, s*	**conquer*** (defeat) *ed, ing, or, s*
composition	*s*	**conquest**	*s*
comprehensive school	*s*	**conscience**	*-smitten, s*
computer	*s*	**conscientious**	*ly, ness*
comrade	*ship, s*	**conscious**	*ly, ness*

*ǿ Drop **e** before adding* ing

* conker
  conquer

20

consent	*ed, ing, s*	**cook**	*ed, ing, er, ery, book, house, s*	
consequence	*s*	**cool**	*ed, ing, er, est, ish, ly, ness, s*	
consequent	*ly*	**co-operate**	*d, ɇing, s*	
conservative	*s*	**co-operation**		
consider	*ed, ing, able, ably, ate, ation, s*	**copper**	*s*	
consist	*ed, ing, s*	**coppice** or **copse**	*s*	
consolation	*-prize, s*	**copy**	*ing*	
conspicuous	*ly, ness*	**cop***ied*	*ies*	
constable	*s*	**coral**	*-island, -reef, s*	
constant	*ly*	**cord**	*s*	
construct	*ed, ing, ion, or, s*	**cordial**	*s*	
consult	*ed, ing, ation, s*	**cordon**	*ed, ing, s*	
consume	*d, ɇing, r, s*	**corduroy**	*s*	
contact	*ed, ing, s*	**core*** (middle of apple, etc.)	*d, ɇing, s*	
contain	*ed, ing, er, s*	**corgi**	*s*	
contemporar*y*	*ies*	**cork**	*ed, ing, screw, s*	
content	*ed, ing, ment, s*	**corn**	*-cob, field, flake, s*	
contest	*ed, ing, ant, s*	**corned beef**		
continent	*al, s*	**corner**	*ed, ing, s*	
continual	*ly*	**cornet**	*s*	
continue	*d, ɇing, s*	**coronation**	*s*	
continuation		**corporal**	*s*	
continuous	*ly, ness*	**corporation**	*s*	
contradict	*ed, ing, ion, s*	**corps*** (group of cadets, etc.) **corps**		
contribute	*d, ɇing, s*	**corpse**	*s*	
contribution	*s*	**correct**	*ed, ing, ion, ly, ness, s*	
control	*led, ling, ler, -column, -lever, s*	**correspond**	*ed, ing, ence, ent, s*	
convalesce	*d, ɇing, nce, nt, s*	**corridor**	*s*	
convenience	*s*	**cosmetic**	*s*	
convenient	*ly*	**cosmonaut**	*s*	
convent	*s*	**cost**	*ing, s*	
conversation	*s*	**costl***y*	*ier, iest, iness*	
convert	*ed, ing, s*	**coster**	*monger, s*	
convey	*ed, ing, ance, s*	**costume**	*s*	
convict	*ed, ing, ion, s*	**cos***y*	*ier, iest, ily, iness, ies*	
convince	*d, ɇing, s*	**cottage**	*s*	
convoy	*ed, ing, s*	**cotton**	*wool, s*	

ɇ Drop **e** before adding *ing*

_* core
   corps

couch	es	**crank**	ed, ing, s
cough	ed, ing, er, -drop, -mixture, s	**crash**	ed, ing, es
could		**crate**	d, ¢ing, ful, s
couldn't (could not)		**crater**	s
council	lor, -chamber, -house, s	**crave**	d, ¢ing, s
count	ed, ing, er, less, -down, s	**crawl**	ed, ing, er, s
counter	ed, ing, -attack, foil, s	**crayon**	ed, ing, s
countess	es	**craze**	d, ¢ing, s
country	ies	**craz**y	ier, iest, ily, iness
county	ies	**creak*** (noise)	ed, ing, s
couple	d, ¢ing, s	**creak**y	ier, iest, ily, iness
coupon	s	**cream**	ed, ing, er, -cake, -cheese, s
courage		**cream**y	ier, iest, ily, iness
courageous	ly, ness	**crease**	d, ¢ing, s
course* (track; direction; of course) s		**create**	d, ¢ing, s
court	ed, ing, ier, room, ship, yard, s	**creature**	s
courtesy	ies	**credit**	able, ed, ing, or, s
cousin	ly, s	**creek*** (small bay, sea-coast inlet) s.	
cove	s	**creep**	ing, er, s
cover	ed, ing, s	**creep**y	ier, iest, ily, iness
cow	boy, hand, herd, hide, shed, s	**cremate**	d, ¢ing, s
coward	s	**crematorium**	s
cowardice		**creosote**	d, ¢ing, s
cowardly	iness	**crept**	
cowslip	s	**crescent**	s
		crest	ed, ing, fallen, s
		crevice	s
cr		**crew**	ed, ing, s
crab	-apple, -pot, s	**crib**	bed, bing, ber, s
crack	ed, ing, er, s	**cricket**	ing, er, -field, s
crackle	d, ¢ing, s	**cried**	
cradle	d, ¢ing, s	**crier**	s
craft	sman, smen, s	**cries**	
crafty	ier, iest, ily, iness	**crime**	s
cram	med, ming, mer, s	**criminal**	s
cramp	ed, ing, s	**crimson**	ed, ing, s
crane	d, ¢ing, -driver, s	**cringe**	d, ¢ing, s

¢ Drop **e** before adding ing

*	course	creak
	coarse	creek

crinkle	*d, øing, s*	**crumple**	*d, øing, s*
crinkly	*ier, iest, iness*	**crunch**	*ed, ing, es*
cripple	*d, øing, s*	**crusade**	*d, øing, r, s*
crisp	*ed, ing, er, est, ly, ness, s*	**crush**	*ed, ing, es*
crispy	*ier, iest, ily, iness*	**crust**	*s*
critic	*al, ally, ism, s*	**crust**y	*ier, iest, ily, iness*
criticize	*d, øing, s*	**crutch**	*es*
croak	*ed, ing, er, s*	**cry**	*ing*
croaky	*ier, iest, ily, iness*	**cr**ied	*ies*
crochet	*ed, ing, -hook, s*	**crypt**	*s*
crockery		**crystal**	*s*
crocodile	*s*		
crocus	*es*		
crook	*s*		**cu**
crooked	*ly, ness*	**Cub Scout**	*s*
crop	*ped, ping, per, s*	**cube**	*d, øing, s*
croquet		**cubicle**	*s*
cross	*ed, ing, er, est, ly, ness, es*	**cuckoo**	*-clock, s*
crossroad	*s*	**cucumber**	*s*
crossword	*s*	**cuddle**	*d, øing, some, s*
crouch	*ed, ing, es*	**cue*** (hint; billiard-stick)	*s*
crow	*ed, ing, bar, s*	**cuff**	*-link, s*
crowd	*ed, ing, s*	**cul-de-sac**	**culs-de-sac**
crown	*ed, ing, s*	**culprit**	*s*
crucify	*ing*	**cultivate**	*d, øing, s*
crucified	*ies*	**cultivation**	
crucifix	*es*	**cunning**	*ly*
crucifixion	*s*	**cup**	*ful, s*
crude	*r, st, ly, ness*	**cupboard**	*s*
cruel	*ler, lest, ly*	**curate**	*s*
cruelty	*ies*	**curator**	*s*
cruet	*s*	**curb*** (hold back)	*ed, ing, s*
cruise	*d, øing, r, s*	**curdle**	*d, øing, s*
crumb	*s*	**cure**	*d, øing, s*
crumble	*d, øing, s*	**curio**	*s*
crumbly	*ier, iest, iness*	**curiosit**y	*ies*
crumpet	*s*	**curious**	*ly, ness*

ø Drop **e** before adding *ing*

```
        cue     curb
  *
        queue   kerb
```

curl	ed, ing, er, s
curl y	ier, iest, ily, iness
currant* (fruit)	-bread, -bun, -cake, s
current* (flow of water, air, etc.)	s
curr y	ied, ies
curse	d, ǿing, s
curt	ly, ness
curtain	ed, ing, s
curtsy	ing
curts ied	ies
curve	d, ǿing, s
cushion	s
custard	-powder, -pie, s
custom	s
customer	s
cut	ting, ter, -price, -rate, -throat, s
cutlass	es
cutlery	

cy

cycle	d, ǿing, -clip, s
cyclist	s
cyclone	s
cygnet* (young swan)	s
cylinder	s
cymbal	ist, s
cypress	es

da

dab	bed, bing, ber, s
dabble	d, ǿing, r, s
dachshund	s
dad	s
dadd y	ies
daffodil	s

daft	er, est, ly, ness
dagger	s
dahlia	s
dail y	ies
daint y	ier, iest, ily, iness, ies
dair y	ies
dais y	ies
dale	s
Dalmatian	s
dam	med, ming, s
damage	d, ǿing, s
dame	s
damp	ed, ing, er, est, ly, ness, s
dampen	ed, ing, er, s
damson	-tree, s
dance	d, ǿing, r, -band, -floor, s
dandelion	s
danger	s
dangerous	ly
dangle	d, ǿing, s
dank	er, est, ly, ness
dapple	d, ǿing, -grey, s
dare	d, ǿing, -devil, s
dark	er, est, ly, ness
darken	ed, ing, s
darling	s
darn	ed, ing, er, s
dart	ed, ing, -board, s
dash	ed, ing, es
date	d, ǿing, -stamp, -palm, s
daub	ed, ing, er, s
daughter	s
dawdle	d, ǿing, r, s
dawn	ed, ing, s
day	break, dream, light, time, s
daze	d, ǿing, s
dazzle	d, ǿing, r, s

ǿ Drop **e** before adding *ing*

*	currant	cygnet
	current	signet

de

de	
dead	-beat, -end, -heat, line, lock, ness
deaden	ed, ing, er, s
deadly	ier, iest, iness
deaf	-aid, er, est, ly, ness
deafen	ed, ing, s
deal	ing, er, s
dealt	
dear* (beloved; costly)	er, est, ly, ness, s
death	ly, -bed, -blow, -rate, -ray, -trap, s
debate	d, ∅ing, r, s
debris	
debt	or, s
decay	ed, ing, s
deceit	ful, fully, s
deceive	d, ∅ing, r, s
December	s
decent	ly
decide	d, dly, ∅ing, s
decimal	s
decipher	ed, ing, s
decision	s
deck	ed, ing, -chair, s
declare	d, ∅ing, s
decline	d, ∅ing, s
decorate	d, ∅ing, s
decoration	s
decorator	s
decrease	d, ∅ing, s
deduct	ed, ing, ion, s
deed	s
deep	er, est, ly, ness
deepen	ed, ing, s
deer* (animal)	skin, stalker, -park, **deer**
defeat	ed, ing, s
defect	ive, s
defence	less, lessly, s

defend	ed, ing, er, s
defiant	ly
definite	ly
degree	s
delay	ed, ing, s
deliberate	ly, ness, d, ∅ing, s
delicacy	ies
delicate	ly, ness
delicious	ly, ness
delight	ed, ing, s
delightful	ly, ness
deliver	ed, ing, ance, s
delivery	ies
deluge	d, ∅ing, s
demand	ed, ing, s
demolish	ed, ing, es
demon	s
demonstrate	d, ∅ing, s
demonstration	s
demonstrator	s
dense	r, st, ly, ness
dent	ed, ing, s
dentist	s
deny	ing
denied	ies
depart	ed, ing, ure, s
department	s
depend	ed, ing, able, ent, s
deport	ed, ing, ation, s
deposit	ed, ing, or, s
depot	s
depth	-charge, s
deputy	ies
derail	ed, ing, ment, s
derelict	s
descant	-recorder, s
descend	ed, ing, ant, s

∅ Drop **e** before adding *ing*

* dear
  deer

di

descent	*s*	**di**	
describe	*d, e̶ing, s*	**diagram**	*s*
description	*s*	**dial**	*led, ling, ler, s*
desert (sandy place)	*s*	**dialect**	*s*
desert* (run away)	*ed, ing, ion, er, s*	**dialogue**	*s*
deserve	*d, e̶ing, s*	**diameter**	*s*
design	*ed, ing, er, s*	**diamond**	*s*
desire	*d, e̶ing, s*	**diar**y	*ies*
desk	*s*	**dictate**	*d, e̶ing, s*
desolate	*d, e̶ing, ly, ness, s*	**dictation**	*s*
despair	*ed, ing, ingly, s*	**dictionar**y	*ies*
despatch or **dispatch**	*ed, ing, es*	**didn't** (did not)	
desperate	*ly, ness*	**die*** (small spotted cube)	**dice**
desperation		**die*** (lose life)	*s*
despise	*d, e̶ing, s*	**died*** (lost life)	
despite		**dying*** (losing life)	
dessert* (fruit, pudding, etc.)	*-spoon, s*	**diet**	*ed, ing, ician, s*
destination	*s*	**differ**	*ed, ing, ence, s*
destroy	*ed, ing, er, s*	**different**	*ly*
destruction		**difficult**	
destructive	*ly, ness*	**difficult**y	*ies*
detach	*ed, ing, es*	**dig**	*ging, ger, s*
detail	*ed, ing, s*	**digest**	*ed, ing, ion, ive, s*
detain	*ed, ing, s*	**dignif**y	*ied, ies*
detect	*ed, ing, ion, or, s*	**dignity**	
detective	*s*	**dike** or **dyke**	*s*
detention	*s*	**dilapidated**	
determination		**dilute**	*d, e̶ing, s*
determine	*d, e̶ing, s*	**dim**	*med, ming, mer, mest, ly, ness, s*
detest	*able, ed, ing, s*	**dimension**	*s*
develop	*ed, ing, er, ment, s*	**dimple**	*d, e̶ing, s*
device	*s*	**dine**	*d, e̶ing, r, s*
devil	*ish, ry, ment, s*	**dining**	*-car, -hall, -room, -table*
devise	*d, e̶ing, s*	**dingh**y	*ies*
devote	*d, e̶ing, s*	**ding**y	*ier, iest, ily, iness*
devour	*ed, ing, er, s*	**dinner**	*-hour, -service, -table, -time, s*
dew* (moisture)	*y, -drop, -fall, -pond, s*	**dinosaur**	*s*

e̶ Drop **e** before adding *ing*

*	desert	dew		die	died	dying
	dessert	due		dye	dyed	dyeing
		Jew				

dip	*ped, ping, per, s*	**dismal**	*ly, ness*
diploma	*s*	**dismantle**	*d, ∅ing, s*
direct	*ed, ing, ly, ness, ive, or, s*	**dismay**	*ed, ing, s*
direction	*-finder, s*	**dismiss**	*ed, ing, es*
director *y*	*ies*	**dismount**	*ed, ing, s*
dirt	*-track*	**disobedience**	
dirt *ied*	*ier, iest, ily, iness, ies*	**disobedient**	*ly*
dirty	*ing*	**disobey**	*ed, ing, s*
disable	*d, ∅ing, ment, s*	**disorder**	*ly, s*
disadvantage	*s*	**dispatch** or **despatch**	*ed, ing, es*
disagree	*able, d, ing, ment, s*	**dispensar** *y*	*ies*
disappear	*ed, ing, ance, s*	**dispense**	*d, ∅ing, r, s*
disappoint	*ed, ing, ment, s*	**display**	*ed, ing, s*
disarm	*ed, ing, ament, s*	**displease**	*d, ∅ing, s*
disarrange	*d, ∅ing, ment, s*	**dispute**	*d, ∅ing, s*
disaster	*s*	**disqualify**	*ing*
disastrous	*ly*	**disqualif** *ied*	*ies, ication*
disc or **disk**	*s*	**dissatisfy**	*ing*
discharge	*d, ∅ing, s*	**dissatisf** *ied*	*ies, action*
disciple	*s*	**dissolve**	*d, ∅ing, s*
discipline	*d, ∅ing, s*	**distance**	*s*
discontent	*ed, edly, ment, s*	**distant**	*ly*
discothèque or **disco**	*-club, -dancing, s*	**distinct**	*ion, ive, ly, ness*
discourage	*d, ∅ing, ment, s*	**distinguish**	*able, ed, ing, es*
discover	*ed, ing, er, s*	**distract**	*ed, ing, ion, s*
discover *y*	*ies*	**distress**	*ed, ing, es*
discuss	*ed, ing, es*	**disribute**	*d, ∅ing, s*
discussion	*s*	**district**	*s*
disease	*d, s*	**disturb**	*ed, ing, ance, s*
disgrace	*d, ∅ing, s*	**ditch**	*ed, ing, es*
disgraceful	*ly, ness*	**divan**	*s*
disguise	*d, ∅ing, s*	**dive**	*d, ∅ing, r, s*
disgust	*ed, ing, s*	**divert**	*ed, ing, s*
dish	*ed, ing, es*	**divide**	*d, ∅ing, r, s*
dishearten	*ed, ing, s*	**division**	*s*
dishonest	*ly, y*	**divorce**	*d, ∅ing, e, s*
dislike	*able, d, ∅ing, s*	**dizz** *y*	*ier, iest, ily, iness*

∅ Drop **e** before adding *ing*

do   dr

do		dr	
docile	*ly*	**drab**	*ber, best, ly, ness*
dock	*ed, ing, er, yard, s*	**drag**	*ged, ging, -net, s*
doctor	*s*	**dragon**	*s*
document	*ed, ing, s*	**dragonfl** *y*	*ies*
dodge	*d, ɇing, r, s*	**drain**	*age, ed, ing, -pipe, s*
doe* (female animal)	*s*	**drake**	*s*
does		**drama**	*tic, tist, s*
doesn't (does not)		**dramatize**	*d, ɇing, s*
doing	*s*	**drank**	
dole	*d, ɇing, ful, fully, s*	**drape**	*d, ɇing, s*
doll	*s*	**draper**	*s*
dollar	*s*	**draper** *y*	*ies*
dolphin	*s*	**drastic**	*ally*
domestic	*ally, s*	**draught**	*sman, smen, -board, s*
domesticate	*d, ɇing, s*	**draught** *y*	*ier, iest, ily, iness*
domino	*es*	**draw**	*n, ing, er, s*
donate	*d, ɇing, s*	**drawbridge**	*s*
donation	*s*	**drawer**	*s*
done		**drawing**	*-board, -paper, -pin, -room, s*
donkey	*s*	**dread**	*ed, ing, s*
don't (do not)		**dreadful**	*ly, ness*
doom	*ed, ing, sday, s*	**dream**	*ed, ing, land, like, er, s*
door	*bell, keeper, mat, step, way, s*	**dreamt** or **dreamed**	
dormitor *y*	*ies*	**dream** *y*	*ier, iest, ily, iness*
dose	*d, ɇing, s*	**drear** *y*	*ier, iest, ily, iness*
dot	*ted, ting, s*	**dredge**	*d, ɇing, r, s*
double	*d, ɇing, -jointed, -decker, s*	**drench**	*ed, ing, es*
doubt	*ed, ing, less, er, s*	**dress**	*ed, ing, es*
doubtful	*ly, ness*	**dresser**	*s*
dough* (moist flour)	*boy, nut, y*	**dressing**	*-gown, -case, -room, -table, s*
douse or **dowse**	*d, ɇing, s*	**dressmaker**	*s*
dove	*cote, s*	**drew**	
dowd *y*	*ier, iest, ily, iness*	**dribble**	*d, ɇing, r, s*
down	*stairs, hill, fall, pour, ward, s*	**drift**	*ed, ing, er, s*
doze	*d, ɇing, s*	**drill**	*ed, ing, er, s*
dozen	*s* or **dozen**	**drink**	*able, ing, er, s*

ɇ Drop **e** before adding *ing*

*   doe
      dough

du   dw   dy

drip	*ped, ping, s*
drive	*ẹing, r, way, s*
driven	
drivel	*led, ling, ler, s*
drizzle	*d, ẹing, s*
drizzly	*ier, iest, iness*
dromedary	*ies*
drone	*d, ẹing, s*
droop	*ed, ing, s*
drop	*ped, ping, per, let, s*
drought	*s*
drove	
drown	*ed, ing, s*
drowse	*d, ẹing, s*
drowsy	*ier, iest, ily, iness*
drudgery	
drug	*ged, ging, gist, -addict, store, s*
drum	*med, ming, mer, -major, stick, s*
drunk	*ard, s*
drunken	*ly, ness*
dry	*ing, ness*
dried	*ier, iest, ies*
dryer or **drier** (noun)	*s*
dryly or **drily**	

du

dual* (two; double)	
duchess	*es*
duck	*ed, ing, ling, s*
due* (expected; owing)	*s*
duel* (a fight)	*led, ling, list, s*
duet	*s*
duffel or **duffle**	*-bag, -coat, s*
dug	*-out*
duke	*dom, s*
dull	*ed, ing, er, est, ish, y, ness, s*

duly	
dumb	*er, est, ly, ness*
dummy	*ies*
dump	*ed, ing, s*
dumpling	*s*
dunce	*s*
dungarees	
dungeon	*s*
duplicate	*d, ẹing, s*
durable	*ness*
duration	
during	
dusk	
dusky	*ier, iest, ily, iness*
dust	*ed, ing, man, men, bin, pan, er, s*
dusty	*ier, iest, ily, iness*
dutiful	*ly, ness*
duty	*ies*

dw

dwarf	*ed, ing, s* or **dwarves**
dwell	*ed, ing, er, s*
dwelling	*-house, -place, s*
dwelt or **dwelled**	
dwindle	*d, ẹing, s*

dy

dye* (colour)	*r, s*
dyed* (coloured)	
dyeing* (colouring)	
dying* (losing life)	
dyke or **dike**	*s*
dynamic	*al, ally, s*
dynamite	*d, ẹing, s*
dynamo	*s*

ẹ Drop e before adding ing

*	due	dual		dye	dyed	dyeing
	dew	duel		die	died	dying
	Jew	jewel				

ea

each	
eager	ly, ness
eagle	t, s
ear	ache, -drum, phone, -plug, -ring, s
earwig	s
earl	dom, s
earl y	ier, iest, iness
earn* (be paid)	ed, ing, er, s
earnt or **earned**	
earnest	ly, ness
earth	quake, worm, work, s
earthen	ware
ease	d, ɇing, s
eas y	ier, iest, ily, iness
easel	s
east	ern, erly, ward, wards
Easter	-egg, s
eat	able, en, ing, er s
eavesdrop	ped, ping, per, s

ec

eccentric	s
echo	ed, ing, es
éclair	s
eclipse	d, ɇing, s
economic	al, ally, s
economize	d, ɇing, s
econom y	ies

ed

eddy	ing
edd ied	ies
edge	d, ɇing, ways, wise, s
edible	

ed

edit	ed, ing, s
edition	s
editor	ial, s
educate	d, ɇing, s
education	al, ally, alist, ist

ee

eel	s
eer ie or **eer** y	ier, iest, ily, iness

ef

effect	ed, ing, s
effective	ly, ness
efficiency	
efficient	ly
effig y	ies
effort	less, lessly, s

eg

egg	-cup, -shell, -spoon, -timer, s

ei

eiderdown	s
either	

el

elaborate	d, ɇing, ly, ness, s
elapse	d, ɇing, s
elastic	ally, ity
elbow	ed, ing, s
elder	ly, s
eldest	
elect	ed, ing, ion, or, s

ɇ Drop **e** before adding *ing*

em

en

electric	al, ally, s
electrician	s
electricity	
electrocute	d, ~~e~~ing, s
elegant	ly
elephant	s
elevator	s
elf	in, ish, **elves**
eligible	
eliminate	d, ~~e~~ing, s
elimination	s
Elizabethan	s
elm	-tree, s
elocution	ist
elope	d, ~~e~~ing, ment, s
else	where

em

embankment	s
embark	ed, ing, ation, s
embarrass	ed, ing, es
embarrassment	s
emblem	s
embrace	d, ~~e~~ing, s
embroider	ed, ing, s
embroider y	ies
emerald	s
emerge	d, ~~e~~ing, s
emergenc y	ies
emigrate	d, ~~e~~ing, s
emperor	s
empire	s
employ	ed, ing, ment, ee, er, s
empress	es
empty	ing
empt ied	ier, iest, ily, iness, ies

en

enable	d, ~~e~~ing, s
enamel	led, ling, s
encamp	ed, ing, ment, s
enchant	ed, ing, ment, s
encircle	d, ~~e~~ing, ment, s
enclose	d, ~~e~~ing, s
enclosure	s
encore	d, ~~e~~ing, s
encounter	ed, ing, s
encourage	d, ~~e~~ing, ment, s
encyclop(a)edia	s
end	ed, ing, less, lessly, s
endanger	ed, ing, s
endeavour	ed, ing, s
endure	d, ~~e~~ing, s
endurance	s
enem y	ies
energetic	ally
energ y	ies
enforce	d, ~~e~~ing, ment, s
engage	d, ~~e~~ing, ment, s
engine	-driver, -room, s
engineer	ed, ing, s
engrave	d, ~~e~~ing, r, s
engulf	ed, ing, s
enjoy	able, ed, ing, ment, s
enlarge	d, ~~e~~ing, r, ment, s
enlist	ed, ing, ment, s
enormous	ly, ness
enough	
enquire or **inquire**	d, ~~e~~ing, r, s
enquir y or **inquir** y	ies
enrage	d, ~~e~~ing, s
enrol	led, ling, ment, s
entangle	d, ~~e~~ing, ment, s
enter	ed, ing, s

~~e~~ Drop **e** before adding *ing*

ep eq er   es ev

enterprise	*s*
entertain	*ed, ing, ment, er, s*
enthusiasm	*s*
enthusiastic	*ally*
entire	*ly, ness*
entitle	*d, ∅ing, ment, s*
entrance	*s*
entry	*ies*
envelope	*s*
envious	*ly, ness*
environment	*al, alist, s*
envy	*ing*
envied	*ies*

ep

epidemic	*s*
epilogue	*s*
episode	*s*

eq

equal	*led, ling, ly, s*
equalize	*d, ∅ing, r, s*
equator	*ial*
equip	*ped, ping, ment, s*
equivalent	*ly*

er

erase	*d, ∅ing, r, s*
erect	*ed, ing, ion, s*
err	*ed, ing, ant, s*
errand	*s*
erratic	*ally*
error	*s*
erupt	*ed, ing, ion, s*

es

escalator	*s*
escapade	*s*
escape	*d, ∅ing, r, s*
escort	*ed, ing, s*
Eskimo	*s* or *es* or **Eskimo**
especial	*ly*
espionage	
esplanade	*s*
essay	*ist, s*
essence	*s*
essential	*ly, s*
establish	*ed, ing, es*
establishment	*s*
estate	*s*
estimate	*d, ∅ing, s*
estuary	*ies*

ev

evacuate	*d, ∅ing, s*
evacuation	*s*
evade	*d, ∅ing, s*
evaporate	*d, ∅ing, s*
eve	*s*
even	*ed, ing, ly, ness, s*
evening	*s*
event	*ful, less, s*
eventual	*ly*
ever	*green, lasting, more*
every	*body, one, thing, where*
evict	*ed, ing, ion, s*
evidence	*s*
evident	*ly*
evil	*ly, ness, s*
evolve	*d, ∅ing, s*
evolution	*s*

∅ Drop **e** before adding *ing*

ex

ex	
exact	ly, ness
exaggerate	d, ∉ing, s
examination	s
examine	d, ∉ing, r, s
examiner	s
example	s
exasperate	d, ∉ing, s
excavate	d, ∉ing, s
excavation	s
exceed	ed, ing, ingly, s
excel	led, ling, s
excellent	ly
except* (leaving out)	ed, ing, s
exception	al, ally, s
excess	ive, ively, es
exchange	d, ∉ing, able, s
excitable	
excite	d, dly, ∉ing, ment, s
exclaim	ed, ing, s
exclude	d, ∉ing, s
exclusive	ly, ness
excursion	s
excuse	d, ∉ing, s
execute	d, ∉ing, s
execution	er, s
exercise	d, ∉ing, s
exert	ed, ing, ion, s
exhaust	ed, ing, ion, ible, ive, -pipe, s
exhibit	ed, ing, or, s
exhibition	s
exile	d, ∉ing, s
exist	ed, ing, ence, ent, s
exit	s
expand	ed, ing, s
expanse	s
expansion	s

expect	ed, ing, ant, ation, s
expedition	s
expel	led, ling, s
expense	s
expensive	ly, ness
experience	d, ∉ing, s
experiment	ed, ing, al, ally, s
expert	ise, ly, ness, s
expire	d, ∉ing, s
explain	ed, ing, s
explanation	s
explode	d, ∉ing, s
exploit	s
exploration	s
explore	d, ∉ing, r, s
explosion	s
explosive	s
export	ed, ing, er, s
expose	d, ∉ing, s
exposure	s
express	ed, ing, es
expression	s
exquisite	ly, ness
extend	ed, ing, s
extension	s
extensive	ly, ness
extent	
exterior	s
extinct	ion
extinguish	ed, ing, es
extra	s
extract	ed, ing, ion, s
extraordinar y	ily, iness
extravagance	s
extravagant	ly
extreme	ly, s
extricate	d, ∉ing, s

∉ Drop ● before adding *ing*

* except
  accept

ey

eye   *d, ball, brow, lid, sight, sore, s*
eyeing or **eying**
eyelash   *es*

fa

fable   *s*
fabulous   *ly, ness*
face *d, ∮ing, -cloth, -flannel, s*
fact   *s*
factor *y*   *ies*
fade   *d, ∮ing, s*
faggot   *s*
fail   *ed, ing, ure, s*
faint *er, est, ish, ly, ness, ed, ing, s*
fair* *er, est, ish, ly, ness, ground, s*
fair *y*   *ies*
faith   *s*
faithful   *ly, ness*
fake   *d, ∮ing, s*
falcon   *er, s*
fall   *en, ing, s*
false   *hood, r, st, ly, ness*
falter   *ed, ing, s*
fame   *d*
familiar   *ity, ly*
famil *y*   *ies*
famine   *s*
famish   *ed, ing, es*
famous   *ly*
fan *ned, ning, ner, -belt, light, tail, s*
fancy   *ing*
fanc *ied ier, iest, ies, iful, ifully*
fantastic   *ally*
far *ther,* thest, -away, -off, -fetched*
fare* (price of journey; food) *s*

fe

farewell   *s*
farm *ed, ing, er, -house, yard, s*
fascinate   *d, ∮ing, s*
fashion   *able, ably, ed, ing, s*
fast   *er, est, ness, ed, ing, s*
fasten   *ed, ing, er, s*
fat   *ted, ter, test, ness, s*
fatten   *ed, ing, s*
fatt *y*   *ier, iest, iness*
fatal   *ly*
fate* (destiny)   *d, ful, s*
father* (parent)   *less, ly, s*
fathom   *ed, ing, s*
fatigue   *d, ∮ing, s*
fault   *ed, ing, less, lessly, s*
fault *y*   *ier, iest, ily, iness*
favour   *able, ably, ed, ing, itism, s*
favourite   *s*
fawn   *ed, ing, s*

fe

fear   *ed, ing, some, s*
fearful   *ly, ness*
fearless   *ly, ness*
feast   *ed, ing, s*
feat* (difficult deed)   *s*
feather *ed, ing, y, -bed, -duster, s*
feature   *d, ∮ing, s*
February   *s*
fed
fee   *s*
feeble   *r, st, ness*
feebly
feed   *ing, er, s*
feel   *ing, er, s*
feet* (pl. of foot)

*∮ Drop **e** before adding* ing

*	fair	farther	fate	feat
	fare	father	fête	feet

fi

feign	*ed, ing, s*	**fiend**	*ish, s*
fell	*ed, ing, s*	**fierce**	*r, st, ly, ness*
fellow	*ship, s*	**fier** *y*	*ier, iest, ily, iness*
felt		**fight**	*ing, er, s*
female	*s*	**figure**	*d, ɇing, s*
feminine	*s*	**file**	*d, ɇing, s*
fence	*d, ɇing, r, s*	**fill**	*ed, ing, er, s*
fend	*ed, ing, er, s*	**fillet**	*ed, ing, s*
fern	*s*	**film** *ed, ing, -set, -star, -studio, s*	
ferocious	*ly, ness*	**filter** *ed, ing, -bed, -paper, -tip, s*	
ferocity		**filth**	
ferret	*ed, ing, er, s*	**filth** *y*	*ier, iest, ily, iness*
ferry	*-boat, ing, man, men*	**final**	*ly, ist, s*
ferr *ied*	*ies*	**finch**	*es*
fertile	*ly*	**find*** (found)	*ing, er, s*
fertilize	*d, ɇing, r, s*	**fine**	*d,* ɇing, s*
fester	*ed, ing, s*	**fine**	*r, st, ly, ness*
festival	*s*	**finger** *ed, ing, -mark, -nail, -print, tip, s*	
festive	*ly*	**finish**	*ed, ing, es*
festivit *y*	*ies*	**fiord** or **fjord**	*s*
fetch	*ed, ing, es*	**fir***	*-cone, -tree, s*
fête* (entertainment; festival) *d, ɇing, s*		**fire**	*d, ɇing, man, men, place, work, s*
feud	*s*	**fire**	*-alarm, -brigade, -engine, -escape, s*
feudal	*ism*	**fire**	*-drill, -extinguisher, side, -station, s*
fever	*ish, ishly, s*	**firm**	*er, est, ly, ness, s*
few	*er, est*	**first**	*ly, -aid, -class, -floor, hand, -rate, s*
		fish *ed, ing, -meal, -paste, y, es or* **fish**	
		fisher	*man, men, s*
## fi		**fishing**	*-boat, -line, -net, -rod, -tackle*
		fishmonger	*s*
fiancé* (masc.)	*s*	**fist**	*s*
fiancée* (fem.)	*s*	**fit** *ted, ting, ter, test, ful, ly, ness, ment, s*	
fibre	*glass, -tip, s*	**fix**	*ed, ing, es*
fiction	*al*	**fixture**	*s*
fictitious	*ly, ness*	**fizz**	*ed, ing, es*
fiddle	*d, ɇing, r, stick, s*	**fizz** *y*	*ier, iest, ily, iness*
fidget	*ed, ing, y, s*	**fizzle**	*d, ɇing, s*
field *ed, ing, sman, smen, er, s*			

ɇ Drop **e** before adding *ing*

*	fête	fiancé	find	fir
	fate	fiancée	fined	fur

fl	
flag ged, ging, -day, -pole, -staff, s	
flagon s	
flake d, ǿing, s	
flame d, ǿing, -thrower, s	
flamingo es or s	
flan s	
flank ed, ing, s	
flannel s	
flap ped, ping, per, jack, s	
flare d, ǿing, s	
flash ed, ing, es	
flash y ier, iest, ily, iness	
flask s	
flat ter, test, ly, ness, let, s	
flatten ed, ing, s	
flatter ed, ing, y, er, s	
flavour ed, ing, less, s	
flaw ed, less, s	
flea* (insect) -bite, -bitten, s	
fleck ed, ing, s	
fledg(e)ling s	
fled	
flee* (run away) ing, s	
fleece d, ǿing, s	
fleec y ier, iest, ily, iness	
fleet ing, er, est, ly, ness, s	
flesh -coloured, -wound	
flew* (fly)	
flex ible, ibility, ed, ing, es	
flick ed, ing, s	
flicker ed, ing, s	
flier or **flyer** s	
flight -deck, -recorder, -test, s	
flims y ier, iest, ily, iness	
flinch ed, ing, es	
fling ing, s	

flint lock, stone, s	
flint y ier, iest, ily, iness	
flip ped, ping, per, s	
flirt ed, ing, ation, s	
flit ted, ting, s	
float ed, ing, er, s	
flock ed, ing, s	
flog ged, ging, s	
flood ed, ing, gate, lit, -lighting, -light, s	
floor ed, ing, -board, -cloth, -show, s	
flop ped, ping, s	
flopp y ier, iest, ily, iness	
floral ly	
florist s	
flounder ed, ing, s	
flour* (ground wheat) ed, ing, y, s	
flourish ed, ing, es	
flow ed, ing, s	
flower* ed, ing, y, -bed, -garden, -pot, s	
flown	
flu* (influenza)	
flue* (chimney-pipe) -pipe, s	
fluent ly	
fluff ed, ing, s	
fluff y ier, iest, ily, iness	
fluid s	
fluke d, ǿing, s	
flung	
flurry ing	
flurr ied ies	
flush ed, ing, es	
fluster ed, ing, s	
flute -player, s	
flutter ed, ing, s	
fl y ies	
flyer or **flier** s	
flying -fish, -machine, -saucer, -squad	

ǿ Drop **e** before adding ing

* flea	flew		flour
flee	flue		flower
	flu		

fo

fo		**forever**	*more*
foal	*ed, ing, s*	**forfeit**	*ed, ing, ure, s*
foam	*ed, ing, -rubber, s*	**forgave**	
foamy	*ier, iest, iness*	**forge**	*d, ∉ing, r, s*
fo'c'sle or **forecastle**	*s*	**forger**y	*ies*
focus	*ed, ing, es* or **foci**	**forget**	*ting, -me-not, s*
foe	*s*	**forgetful**	*ly, ness*
fog	*ged, ging, -horn, -lamp, -signal, s*	**forgot**	*ten*
foggy	*ier, iest, ily, iness*	**forgive**	*n, ∉ing, ness, s*
foil	*ed, ing, s*	**fork**	*ed, ing, s*
fold	*ed, ing, er, s*	**forlorn**	*ly, ness*
foliage		**form**	*ed, ing, ation, s*
folk	*-dance, lore, -song, -tale, s* or **folk**	**former**	*ly*
follow	*ed, ing, er, s*	**formidable**	
folly	*ies*	**formula**	*e* or *s*
fond	*er, est, ly, ness*	**fort*** (castle)	*s*
fondle	*d, ∉ing, s*	**forth*** (forward)	*coming*
food	*stuff, store, s*	**fortification**	*s*
fool	*ed, ing, hardy, s*	**fortify**	*ing*
foolish	*ly, ness*	**fortif**ied	*ies*
foot	*ing, hold, path, sore, work,* **feet**	**fortnight**	*ly*
football	*er, s*	**fortress**	*es*
footprint	*s*	**fortunate**	*ly*
footstep	*s*	**fortune**	*-teller, s*
for*		**forward**	*ed, ing, ly, ness, s*
forbad or **forbade**		**fossil**	*s*
forbid	*den, ding, s*	**fought*** (fight)	
force	*d, ∉ing, s*	**foul*** (dirty)	*ed, ing, er, est, ly, ness, s*
ford	*ed, ing, s*	**found**	*ed, ing, er*
fore*(front)	*arm, ground, most, man, men*	**foundation**	*-stone, s*
forecast	*ing, er, s*	**foundr**y	*ies*
forehead	*s*	**fountain**	*-pen, s*
foreign		**fowl*** (bird)	*s* or **fowl**
foreigner	*s*	**fox**	*es, hounds, hunting, y*
forest	*ry, er, s*	**foxglove**	*s*
foretell	*ing, er, s*	**fox-terrier**	*s*
foretold		**foyer**	*s*

*∉ Drop **e** before adding* ing

*	for		fort	forth	foul
	fore		fought	fourth (4th)	fowl
	four (4)				

fr   fu

fr	
fraction	s
fracture	d, ǿing, s
fragile	ly, ness
fragment	s
fragrance	s
fragrant	ly
frail	er, est, ly, ty, ness
frame	d, ǿing, r, work, s
franc* (foreign coin)	s
frank* (candid, etc.)	er, est, ly, ness, s
frankincense	
frantic	ally, ly
fraud	s
fray	ed, ing, s
freak	ish, s
freckle	d, ǿing, s
free	d, ing, r, st, ly, dom, -style, way, s
freeze* (ice; cold)	r, s
freezing	-point
freight	er, s
frequent	ly, ed, ing, s
fresh	er, est, ly, ness
freshen	ed, ing, er, s
fret	ted, ting, ful, fully, s
fret	work, saw, s
friar	s
Friday	s
fried	
friend	ship, s
friendly	ier, iest, iness
frieze* (wall decoration)	s
frigate	s
fright	s
frighten	ed, ing, s
frightful	ly, ness
frill	ed, ing, y, s

fringe	d, ǿing, s
frisk	ed, ing, s
frisky	ier, iest, ily, iness
fritter	ed, ing, s
frivolous	ly, ness
frizz	ed, ing, es
frizzy	ier, iest, ily, iness
frock	s
frog	-spawn, s
frolic	ked, king, some, s
front	ed, ing, s
frontier	s
frost	ed, ing, -bite, -bitten, s
frosty	ier, iest, ily, iness
froth	ed, ing, s
frothy	ier, iest, ily, iness
frown	ed, ing, s
froze	n
frugal	ity, ly
fruit	-cake, -juice, -tree, s
fry	er, ing
fried	ies

fu	
fudge	
fuel	led, ling, s
fugitive	s
fulfil	led, ling, ment, s
full	er, est, y, ness
fumble	d, ǿing, r, s
fume	d, ǿing, s
fun	fair
funny	ier, iest, ily, iness
function	ed, ing, s
fund	s
funeral	s

ǿ Drop **e** before adding *ing*

*	franc	freeze
	frank	frieze

ga

fungus	*es* or **fungi**
funnel	*led, ling, s*
fur* (animal's coat)	*rier, s*
furr *y*	*ier, iest, ily, iness*
furious	*ly, ness*
furl	*ed, ing, s*
furnace	*s*
furnish	*ed, ing, ings, es*
furniture	
furrow	*ed, ing, s*
further	*ed, ing, more, most, s*
furthest	
furtive	*ly, ness*
fur *y*	*ies*
furze	*s*
fuse	*d, ∉ing, s*
fuselage	*s*
fuss	*ed, ing, es*
fuss *y*	*ier, iest, ily, iness*
futile	*ly*
future	*s*
fuzz *y*	*ier, iest, ily, iness*

ga

gabardine or **gaberdine**	
gabble	*d, ∉ing, r, s*
gag	*ged, ging, s*
gaiet *y*	*ies*
gaily	
gain	*ed, ing, s*
gait* (way of walking)	*s*
gala	*s*
galactic	
galax *y*	*ies*
gale	*s*
gallant	*ly, s*

galleon	*s*
galler *y*	*ies*
galley	*-slave, s*
gallon	*s*
gallop	*ed, ing, s*
gallows	
gamble* (bet)	*d, ∉ing, r, s*
gambol* (leap; frisk)	*led, ling, s*
game	*r, st, ly, ness, keeper, s*
gander	*s*
gang	*ed, ing, ster, s*
gangway	*s*
gaol or **jail**	*ed, ing, er, s*
gape	*d, ∉ing, r, s*
garage	*d, ∉ing, s*
garbage	
garden	*ed, ing, er, s*
gargle	*d, ∉ing, s*
garland	*ed, ing, s*
garlic	
garment	*s*
garret	*s*
garrison	*ed, ing, s*
garter	*s*
gas	*sed, sing, es*
gash	*ed, ing, es*
gasp	*ed, ing, s*
gate* (door)	*keeper, post, way, s*
gather	*ed, ing, er, s*
gaud *y*	*ier, iest, ily, iness*
gauge	*d, ∉ing, s*
gauntlet	*s*
gauze	*s*
gave	
gay	*er, est*
gaily	
gaze	*d, ∉ing, r, s*

∉ Drop **e** *before adding* ing

* fur	gait	gamble
fir	gate	gambol

ge gh   gi gl

ge

gear	ed, ing, case, -lever, wheel, s
geese	
Geiger counter	s
gem	s
general	s
generally	
generate	d, ǿing, s
generation	s
generator	s
generosity	
generous	ly
genie	**genii**
genius	es
gentle	r, st, ness, man, men
gently	
genuine	ly, ness
geograph y	ical, ically
geologist	s
geolog y	ical, ically
geometr y	ic, ical, ically
Georgian	s
geranium	s
germ	s
germinate	d, ǿing, s
germination	s
gesticulate	d, ǿing, s
gesture	d, ǿing, s
get	ting, ter, away, s
geyser	s

gh

ghastl y	ier, iest, ily, iness
gherkin	s
ghost	s
ghostl y	ier, iest, ily, iness

gi

giant	-killer, s
gidd y	ier, iest, ily, iness
gift	ed, s
gigantic	ally
giggle	d, ǿing, r, s
gild* (cover with gold)	ed, ing, er, s
gilt* (gold covering)	
ginger	-ale, -beer, bread, -snap, s
gips y or **gyps** y	ies
giraffe	s
girder	s
girl	ish, -friend, s
Girl Guide	s
give	n, ǿing, r, s

gl

glacier	s
glad	der, dest, ly, ness
gladden	ed, ing, s
glade	s
gladiator	s
gladiolus	es or **gladioli**
glamour	
glamorous	ly
glance	d, ǿing, s
glare	d, ǿing, s
glass	es
gleam	ed, ing, s
glean	ed, ing, er, s
glee	ful, fully
glide	d, ǿing, r, s
glimmer	ed, ing, s
glimpse	d, ǿing, s
glint	ed, ing, s
glisten	ed, ing, s

ǿ Drop **e** before adding *ing*

*	gild	gilt
	guild	guilt

gn go   gra

glitter	*ed, ing, s*	**golliwog**	*s*
gloat	*ed, ing, s*	**gondola**	*s*
globe	*-trotter, s*	**gondolier**	*s*
glockenspiel	*s*	**gone**	
gloom		**gong**	*s*
gloom *y*	*ier, iest, ily, iness*	**good**	*-hearted, ly, ness, s*
glor *y*	*ied, ies*	**good-bye**	*s*
glorious	*ly*	**goose**	**geese**
gloss *y*	*ier, iest, ily, iness*	**gooseberr** *y*	*ies*
glove	*-puppet, s*	**gore**	*d, ø̸ing, s*
glow	*ed, ing, -worm, s*	**gorge**	*d, ø̸ing, s*
glue	*d, ø̸ing, y, -pot, s*	**gorgeous**	*ly, ness*
glum	*mer, mest, ly, ness*	**gorilla**	*s*
		gorse	*s*
		gosling	*s*

gn

gnash	*ed, ing, es*
gnat	*-bite, s*
gnaw	*n, ed, ing, er, s*
gnome	*s*

gossip	*ed, ing, er, s*
govern	*ed, ing, or, ment, s*
governess	*es*
gown	*s*

gr

grab	*bed, bing, ber, s*

go

goal	*keeper, -kick, -mouth, -post, s*
goat	*herd, skin, s*
gobble	*d, ø̸ing, r, s*
goblet	*s*
goblin	*s*
god	*son, father, mother, parent, s*
goddess	*es*
godchild	*ren*
goes	
going	*s*
goggle	*d, ø̸ing, s*
gold	*en, -dust, -field, -mine, -smith*
goldfish	*es* or **goldfish**
golf	*ing, -club, -course, -links, er, s*

grace	*d, ø̸ing, s*
graceful	*ly, ness*
gracious	*ly, ness*
grade	*d, ø̸ing, s*
gradient	*s*
gradual	*ly, ness*
grain	*s*
grammar	
gramophone	*s*
grand	*er, est, ly, ness, stand*
grand	*father, pa, mother, ma, parents*
grandad or **grand-dad**	*s*
grandchild	*ren*
grann *y*	*ies*

ø̸ Drop **e** before adding *ing*

grange · s
granite
grant · ed, ing, s
grape · fruit, -vine, s
graph · ed, ing, s
grapple · d, ǿing, s
grasp · ed, ing, s
grass · ed, ing, es
grass y · ier, iest, iness
grasshopper · s
grass-snake · s
grate* (fireplace; rub) · r,* d, ǿing, s
grateful · ly, ness
grating · s
gratitude
grave · r, st, ly, ness
grave · -digger, stone, yard, s
gravel · led, ling, ly, -path, -pit, s
gravit y · ies
grav y · ies
graze · d, ǿing, s
grease · d, ǿing, r, -paint, -proof, s
greas y · ier, iest, ily, iness
great* (large) · er,* est, ly, ness, s
greed
greed y · ier, iest, ily, iness
green · er, est, ly, ness, ery, ish, y, s
greengrocer · s
greenhouse · s
greet · ed, ing, s
grenade · s
grenadier · s
grew
grey · er, est, ly, ness, ish, hound, s
grief · -stricken, s
grievance · s
grieve · d, ǿing, s

grill* (cook) · ed, ing, er, s
grille* (grating) · s
grim · mer, mest, ly, ness
grime
grim y · ier, iest, ily, iness
grin · ned, ning, ner, s
grind · ing, er, stone, s
grip · ped, ping, per, s
gristle
grit · ted, ting, ter, s
gritt y · ier, iest, ily, iness
grizzle · d, ǿing, r, s
groan* (moan) · ed, ing, er, s
grocer · s
grocer y · ies
groom · ed, ing, s
groove · d, ǿing, s
grope · d, ǿing, s
grotesque · ly, ness
grotto · es or s
ground · ed, ing, sheet, sman, smen, s
group · ed, ing, -leader, s
grove · s
grovel · led, ling, ler, s
grow · th, ing, er, s
grown* (got bigger)
grown-up · s
growl · ed, ing, er, s
grub · bed, bing, ber, s
grubb y · ier, iest, ily, iness
grudge · d, ǿing, s
gruel
gruesome · ly, ness
gruff · er, est, ly, ness
grumble · d, ǿing, r, s
grump y · ier, iest, ily, iness
grunt · ed, ing, er, s

ǿ Drop **e** before adding *ing*

* grate   grater   grill   groan
  great   greater   grille   grown

gu gy   ha

gu

guarantee	d, ing, s
guard	ed, ing, sman, smen, room, s
guardian	s
guess	ed,* ing, es, work
guest* (visitor)	-night, -house, -room, s
guide	d, ɇing, -dog, -book, -post, s
guild* (society)	hall, s
guillotine	d, ɇing, s
guilt* (wrongdoing)	less, lessly
guilt y	ier, iest, ily, iness
guinea-pig	s
guitar	ist, s
gulf	s
gull	s
gull y	ies
gulp	ed, ing, s
gum	med, ming, boil, -tree, s
gumm y	ier, iest, iness
gun	ned, ning, ner, nery, man, men, s
gun	fire, point, powder, shot, smith, s
gurgle	d, ɇing, s
gush	ed, ing, es
gust	ed, ing, s
gust y	ier, iest, ily, iness
gut	ted, ting, s
gutter	s
guy	s
guzzle	d, ɇing, r, s

gy

gymkhana	s
gymnasium	s or **gymnasia**
gymnast	ic, s
gymslip	s
gyps y or **gips** y	ies

ha

habit	s
hack	ed, ing, er, s
haddock	s or **haddock**
hadn't (had not)	
hail	ed, ing, er, stone, storm, s
hair*	dresser, -dryer, pin, -slide, -style, s
hair y	ier, iest, iness
hake	s or **hake**
half	-price, -term, -time, -way, **halves**
halfpenn y	ies or **halfpence**
hall* (room; passage)	way, s
hallo or **hello** or **hullo**	ed, ing, s
halo	es or s
halt	ed, ing, s
halve	d, ɇing, s
hamburger	s
hammer	ed, ing, s
hammock	s
hamper	ed, ing, s
hamster	s
hand	ed, ing, bag, work, writing, ful, s
handcuff	ed, ing, s
handicap	ped, ping, per, s
handicraft	
handiwork	
handkerchief	s
handle	d, ɇing, r, -bar, s
handsome	r, st, ly, ness
hand y	ier, iest, ily, iness
hang	ed, ing, -gliding, -glider, s
hangar* (aeroplane shed)	s
hanger* (for clothes, etc.)	s
happen	ed, ing, s
happ y	ier, iest, ily, iness
harbour	ed, ing, -master, s
hard	er, est, ish, ly, ness, -hearted, ware

ɇ Drop **e** before adding ing

*	guessed	guild	guilt		hair	hall	hangar
	guest	gild	gilt		hare	haul	hanger

he

harden	*ed, ing, er, s*
hardship	*s*
hare* (animal)	*s*
hark	*en*
harm	*ed, ing, s*
harmful	*ly, ness*
harmless	*ly, ness*
harness	*ed, ing, es*
harp	*ist, s*
harpoon	*ed, ing, -gun, s*
harsh	*er, est, ly, ness*
hart* (stag)	*s*
harvest	*ed, ing, er, s*
hasn't (has not)	
haste	*d, ∅ing, s*
hasten	*ed, ing, s*
hast y	*ier, iest, ily, iness*
hat	*band, -peg, -pin, stand, -trick, ful, s*
hatch	*ed, ing, es*
hatchet	*s*
hate	*d, ∅ing, r, s*
hateful	*ly, ness*
hatred	
haught y	*ier, iest, ily, iness*
haul* (pull)	*age, ed, ing, ier, s*
haunt	*ed, ing, s*
have	*∅ing*
haven't (have not)	
haversack	*s*
havoc	
haw	*thorn, s*
hawk	*ed, ing, er, s*
hay	*field, maker, making, rick, stack, s*
hazard	*ed, ing, ous, ously, s*
hazel	*nut, -tree, s*
haze	*s*
haz y	*ier, iest, ily, iness*

he

head	*ed, ing, ache, long, light, way, s*
headmaster	*s*
headmistress	*es*
headquarters	
heal* (cure)	*ed, ing, er, s*
health	
health y	*ier, iest, ily, iness*
heap	*ed, ing, s*
hear* (listen)	*ing, s*
heard* (listened)	
heart* (of body)	*ache, -broken, less, s*
hearten	*ed, ing, s*
heart y	*ier, iest, ily, iness*
hearth	*-rug, s*
heat	*ed, edly, ing, er, -stroke, wave, s*
heath	*land, s*
heathen	*s*
heather	*s*
heave	*d, ∅ing, r, s*
heaven	*ly, ward, s*
heav y	*ier, iest, ily, iness*
he'd (he had; he would)	
hedge	*d, ∅ing, hog, row, -sparrow, s*
heed	*ed, ing, ful, less, s*
heel* (back of foot)	*ed, ing, s*
heft y	*ier, iest, ily, iness*
heifer	*s*
height	*s*
heighten	*ed, ing, s*
heir* (one who inherits)	*loom, s*
heiress	*es*
held	
helicopter	*s*
he'll (he will; he shall)	
hello or **hallo** or **hullo**	*ed, ing, s*
helm	*sman, smen, s*

*∅ Drop **e** before adding ing*

* hare	haul	hart	heal	hear	heard	heir
hair	hall	heart	heel	here	herd	air

hi

ho

helmet	s
help	ed, ing, er, s
helpful	ly, ness
helpless	ly, ness
helter-skelter	s
hem	med, ming, -line, s
her	self, s
herald	ed, ing, s
herb	age, al, alist, s
herd* (of cattle, etc.)	ed, ing, sman, s
here* (in this place)	about(s), by, with
here's (here is)	
hermit	age, -crab, s
hero	es
heroic	al, ally, s
heroine	s
heroism	
heron	s
herring	-gull, s or **herring**
he's (he is; he has)	
hesitate	d, øing, s
hesitation	s
hew* (chop; cut)	n, ed, ing, er, s
hexagon	al, s

hi

hibernate	d, øing, s
hibernation	
hiccup	ed, ing, s
hid	den
hide	øing, -and-seek, away, -out, s
hideous	ly, ness
high	er*, est, ly, chair, light, -road, s
highland	er, s
Highness	es
highway	man, men, s

hijack	ed, ing, er, s
hike	d, øing, r, s
hilarious	ly, ness
hill	ock, side, top, s
hill y	ier, iest, iness
him* (he)	self
hinder	ed, ing, s
hindrance	s
hinge	d, øing, s
hint	ed, ing, s
hippopotamus	es or **hippopotami**
hire* (rent)	d, øing, -purchase, r, s
hiss	ed, ing, es
historic	al, ally
histor y	ies
hit	ting, ter, s
hitch	ed, ing, es
hitch-hike	d, øing, r, s
hive	s

ho

hoard* (hidden store)	ed, ing, s
hoarse* (husky)	r, st, ly, ness
hobble	d, øing, s
hobb y	ies
hockey	-stick
hoe	d, ing, s
hog	skin, s
hoist	ed, ing, s
hold	ing, -all, -up, er, s
hole* (hollow place)	d, øing, s
holiday	ed, ing, -camp, -maker, s
hollow	ed, ing, ly, ness, s
holl y	ies
hollyhock	s
holster	s

ø Drop e before adding ing

herd	here	hew	higher	him	hoard	hoarse	hole
heard	hear	hue	hire	hymn	horde	horse	whole

hu

holy* (godly)	*ier, iest, ily, iness, ies*
home	*-grown, -made, work, ward, s*
homeless	*ness*
homely	*ier, iest, iness*
homesick	*ness*
honest	*ly, y*
honey	*-bee, dew, -pot, comb, suckle, s*
honeymoon	*ed, ing, er, s*
honour	*able, ably, ed, ing, s*
hood	*ed, ing, s*
hoof	*beat, mark, s* or **hooves**
hook	*ed, ing, er, s*
hooligan	*ism, s*
hoop	*ed, ing, -la, s*
hoot	*ed, ing, er, s*
hop	*ped, ping, per, s*
hope	*d, ∅ing, s*
hopeful	*ly, ness*
hopeless	*ly, ness*
horde* (crowd)	*s*
horizon	*tal, tally, s*
horn	*s*
hornpipe	*s*
hornet	*s*
horoscope	*s*
horrible	*ness*
horribly	
horrid	*ly, ness*
horrify	*ing*
horrified	*ies*
horror	*-stricken, -struck, s*
horse* (animal)	*back, man, men, shoe, s*
horse-chestnut	*-tree, s*
hose	*d, ∅ing, -pipe, s*
hospital	*s*
hospitality	
host	*s*

hostage	*s*
hostel	*led, ling, ler, s*
hostess	*es*
hostile	*ly*
hot	*ter, test, ly, ness, house, -plate*
hotel	*ier, s*
hound	*ed, ing, s*
hour* (sixty mins.)	*ly, -hand, s*
house	*d, ∅ing, hold, work, keeper, s*
housemaster	*s*
housemistress	*es*
housewife	*wives*
hover	*ed, ing, port, s, craft*
however	
howl	*ed, ing, er, s*

hu

huddle	*d, ∅ing, s*
hue* (colour)	*s*
hug	*ged, ging, s*
huge	*r, st, ly, ness*
hullo or **hallo** or **hello**	*ed, ing, s*
hum	*med, ming, mer, s*
human	*ity, ly*
humble	*d, ∅ing, r, st, ness, s*
humbly	
humid	*ity*
humiliate	*d, ∅ing, s*
humorous	*ly, ness*
humour	*ed, ing, s*
hump	*ed, ing, s*
hunch	*ed, ing, s*
hundred	*th, weight, s*
hung	
hunger	*ed, ing, s*
hungry	*ier, iest, ily, iness*

∅ Drop **e** before adding *ing*

*	holy	horde	horse		hour	hue
	wholly	hoard	hoarse		our	hew

hunt	*ed, ing, sman, smen, er, s*
hurdle	*d, ø̸ing, r, s*
hurl	*ed, ing, er, s*
hurrah or **hurray**	*ed, ing, s*
hurricane	*-lamp, s*
hurry	*ing*
hurr *ied*	*iedly, ies*
hurt	*ing, s*
hurtle	*d, ø̸ing, s*
husband	*s*
hush	*ed, ing, es*
husk *y*	*ier, iest, ily, iness*
hustle	*d, ø̸ing, s*
hutch	*es*

hy

hyacinth	*s*
hydrangea	*s*
hydraulic	*ally, s*
hydrofoil	*s*
hydrogen	
hydroplane	*s*
hyena or **hyaena**	*s*
hygiene	
hygienic	*ally*
hymn* (song of praise)	*al, -book, s*
hypnotism	
hypnotist	*s*
hypnotize	*d, ø̸ing, s*
hysteric	*al, ally, s*

ic

ice	*d, ø̸ing, berg, -cream, -cube, s*
icicle	*s*
ic *y*	*ier, iest, ily, iness*

id

I'd (I would; I should; I had)	
idea	*s*
ideal	*ly, ism, ist, s*
identical	*ly*
identification	
identify	*ing*
identif *ied*	*ies*
identit *y*	*ies*
idiot	*s*
idiotic	*al, ally*
idle* (lazy)	*d, ø̸ing, r, st, ness, s*
idly	
idol* (false god)	*s*
idolize	*d, ø̸ing, s*

ig

igloo	*s*
ignite	*d, ø̸ing, s*
ignorance	
ignorant	*ly*
ignore	*d, ø̸ing, s*

il

I'll (I will)	
ill	*-bred, -mannered, -treated, s*
illness	*es*
illegal	*ly*
illegible	
illiterate	*ly, ness, s*
illuminate	*d, ø̸ing, s*
illumination	*s*
illusion	*ist, s*
illustrate	*d, ø̸ing, s*
illustration	*s*

ø̸ Drop **e** before adding *ing*

*	hymn	idle
	him	idol

im

in

im	
I'm (I am)	
image	s
imaginary	
imagination	s
imagine	d, e̸ing, s
imitate	d, e̸ing, s
imitation	s
immediate	ly, ness
immense	ly, ness
immortal	ity, ly, s
immune	
immunize	d, e̸ing, s
impatience	
impatient	ly
imperfect	ion, ly
impersonate	d, e̸ing, s
impersonation	s
impertinence	s
impertinent	ly
implement	s
implore	d, e̸ing, s
impolite	ly, ness
import	ed, ing, er, s
importance	
important	ly
impose	d, e̸ing, s
impossibility	ies
impossible	
impress	ed, ing, ive, es
impression	able, s
imprison	ed, ing, ment, s
improve	d, e̸ing, ment, s
impudence	
impudent	ly
impure	ly
impurity	ies

in	
inaccurate	ly
inattentive	ly, ness
incapable	
inch	ed, ing, es
incident	al, ally, s
incline	d, e̸ing, s
include	d, e̸ing, s
inclusive	ly, ness
income	s
inconvenience	d, e̸ing, s
inconvenient	ly
incorrect	ly, ness
increase	d, e̸ing, s
incredible	y
incurable	ness, s
indeed	
indefinite	ly, ness
independent	ly
indicate	d, e̸ing, s
indication	s
indicator	s
indigestion	
indignant	ly
indignation	
indistinct	ly, ness
individual	ly, s
indoor	s
industrial	ly
industrious	ly
industry	ies
inexpensive	ly, ness
infant	s
infantry	man, men
infect	ed, ing, ious, ion, s
inferior	ity, ly, s
infirmary	ies

e̸ Drop **e** before adding *ing*

inflammable	*ness*	**inspect**	*ed, ing, ion, or, s*
inflate	*d, ∉ing, s*	**inspiration**	*s*
influence	*d, ∉ing, s*	**inspire**	*d, ∉ing, s*
influenza		**install**	*ed, ing, ation, s*
inform	*ed, ing, ation, er, s*	**instalment**	*s*
infrequent	*ly*	**instance**	*s*
infuriate	*d, ∉ing, s*	**instant**	*aneous, ly*
ingredient	*s*	**instead**	
inhabit	*ed, ing, able, ant, s*	**instinct**	*ive, ively, s*
inhale	*d, ∉ing, s*	**institute**	*d, ∉ing, s*
inherit	*ed, ing, ance, s*	**institution**	*al, s*
initial	*led, ling, s*	**instruct**	*ed, ing, ive, ion, or, s*
inject	*ed, ing, ion, s*	**instrument**	*al, alist, s*
injure	*d, ∉ing, s*	**insufficient**	*ly*
injury	*ies*	**insult**	*ed, ing, s*
ink	*ed, ing, -bottle, -pot, stand, -well, s*	**insurance**	*s*
inky	*ier, iest, iness*	**insure**	*d, ∉ing, s*
inland		**intact**	
inn	*keeper, s*	**intelligence**	
inner	*most*	**intelligent**	*ly*
innings		**intend**	*ed, ing, s*
innocence		**intense**	*ly, ness*
innocent	*ly, s*	**intent**	*ly, ness*
inoculate	*d, ∉ing, s*	**intention**	*al, ally, s*
inoculation	*s*	**intercept**	*ed, ing, ive, ion, or s*
inquire or **enquire**	*d, ∉ing, r, s*	**interest**	*ed, ing, s*
inquiry or **enquir**y	*ies*	**interfere**	*d, ∉ing, nce, s*
inquisitive	*ly, ness*	**interior**	*s*
insane	*ly*	**interlude**	*s*
inscription	*s*	**intermediate**	*ly*
insect	*s*	**international**	*ly*
insensible		**interpret**	*ed, ing, ation, er, s*
insert	*ed, ing, ion, s*	**interrogate**	*d, ∉ing, s*
inside	*s*	**interrupt**	*ed, ing, ion, s*
insist	*ed, ing, ence, ent, s*	**interval**	*s*
insolence		**intervene**	*d, ∉ing, s*
insolent	*ly*	**interview**	*ed, ing, er, s*

∉ Drop **e** before adding *ing*

introduce	*d, ǿing, s*
introduction	*s*
intrude	*d, ǿing, r, s*
invade	*d, ǿing, r, s*
invalid	*ed, ing, s*
invasion	*s*
invent	*ed, ing, ive, ion, or, s*
investigate	*d, ǿing, s*
investigation	*s*
investigator	*s*
invisible	*ness*
invitation	*s*
invite	*d, ǿing, s*
involve	*d, ǿing, s*
inward	*ly, s*

ir

iris	*es*
iron	*ed, ing, monger, work, s*
ironing-board	*s*
irregular	*ity, ly*
irrigate	*d, ǿing, s*
irrigation	
irritable	*y*
irritability	*ies*
irritate	*d, ǿing, s*
irritation	*s*

is

island	*er, s*
isle* (island)	*s*
isn't (is not)	
isolate	*d, ǿing, s*
isolation	
issue	*d, ǿing, s*

it

italic	*s*
itch	*ed, ing, es*
itchy	*ier, iest, iness*
item	*s*
its* (belonging to it)	
it's* (it is)	
itself	

iv

I've (I have)	
ivory	*ies*
ivy	*ies*

ja

jab	*bed, bing, s*
jabber	*ed, ing, s*
jack	*ed, ing, pot, s*
jackdaw	*s*
jacket	*s*
jade	*d, ǿing, s*
jagged	*ly, ness*
jaguar	*s*
jail or **gaol**	*ed, ing, er, s*
jam	*med, ming, my, -pot, -jar, s*
jamboree	*s*
jangle	*d, ǿing, s*
January	*s*
jar	*red, ring, ful, s*
jaunt	*ed, ing, s*
jaunty	*ier, iest, ily, iness*
javelin	*s*
jaw	*-bone, s*
jay	*s*
jazz	*ed, ing, y, es*

ǿ Drop *e* before adding *ing*

* isle / aisle

its / it's

je ji jo   ju

je

jealous	ly
jealous y	ies
jeans	
jeep	s
jeer	ed, ing, s
jell y	ied, ies
jelly-fish	es or **jelly-fish**
jemm y	ies
jerk	ed, ing, s
jerk y	ier, iest, ily, iness
jerkin	s
jersey	s
jest	ed, ing, er, s
jet	ted, ting, -liner, -plane, -fighter, s
jettison	ed, ing, s
jett y	ies
Jew*	ish, s
jewel*	led, ling, ler, -case, s
jewellery or **jewelry**	

ji

jiff y	ies
jig	ged, ging, ger, s
jigsaw puzzle	s
jilt	ed, ing, s
jingle	d, ¢ing, -jangle, s
jiu-jitsu or **ju-jitsu** or **judo**	
jive	d, ¢ing, s

jo

job	less, s
jockey	s
jocular	ity, ly
jodhpurs	

jo (ju column)

jog	ged, ging, ger, s
join	ed, ing, ery, er, s
joint	ed, ing, ly, s
joist	s
joke	d, ¢ing, r, s
jollit y	ies
joll y	ier, iest, ily, iness
jolt	ed, ing, s
jonquil	s
jostle	d, ¢ing, s
jot	ted, ting, ter, s
journal	ism, ist, s
journey	ed, ing, s
joust	ed, ing, s
jovial	ity, ly
joy	s
joyful	ly, ness
joyous	ly, ness

ju

jubilant	ly
jubilation	s
jubilee	s
judge	d, ¢ing, s
judg(e)ment	s
judo or **ju-jitsu** or **jiu-jitsu**	
juggle	d, ¢ing, r, s
juice	s
juic y	ier, iest, ily, iness
July	s
jumble	d, ¢ing, -sale, s
jump	ed, ing, er, -jet, s
jumper	s
jump y	ier, iest, ily, iness
junction	s
June	s

¢ Drop **e** before adding *ing*

*	Jew	jewel
	dew	dual
	due	duel

jungle	*s*
junior	*s*
junk	*-shop, s*
junket	*s*
juror	*s*
jur y	*ies*
just	*ly, ness*
justice	
justify	*ing*
justif ied	*ies*
jut	*ted, ting, s*
juvenile	*s*

ka

kaleidoscope	*s*
kangaroo	*s*
karate	
kayak	*s*

ke

keel	*ed, ing, s*
keen	*er, est, ly, ness*
keep	*ing, er, sake, s*
kennel	*-maid, s*
kept	
kerb* (pavement edge)	*side, stone, s*
kernel* (nut; seed)	*s*
kestrel	*s*
ketchup	
kettle	*-holder, ful, s*
key*	*hole, -ring, s*

kh

khaki	*s*

ki

kick	*ed, ing, -off, er, s*
kid	*skin, s*
kidnap	*ped, ping, per, s*
kidney	*-bean, s*
kill	*ed, ing, er, s*
kiln	*s*
kilogram(me)	*s*
kilometre	*s*
kilt	*s*
kimono	*s*
kin	*sfolk, sman, smen*
kind	*er, est, -hearted, s*
kindl y	*ier, iest, ily, iness*
kindness	*es*
kindergarten	*s*
kindle	*d, ⌀ing, s*
king	*dom, cup, fisher, s*
kink	*ed, ing, y, s*
kiosk	*s*
kipper	*s*
kiss	*ed, ing, es*
kit	*ted, ting, -bag, s*
kitchen	*ette, -maid, s*
kite	*s*
kitten	*s*

kn

knack	*s*
knapsack	*s*
knave* (rogue)	*s*
knead* (work dough)	*ed, ing, s*
knee	*-deep, -high, -cap, s*
kneel	*ed, ing, s*
knelt or **kneeled**	
knew* (know)	

*⌀ Drop **e** before adding* ing

*	kerb	kernel	key		knave	knead	knew
	curb	colonel	quay		nave	need	new

la

knife	d, øing, -edge, -point, **knives**
knight* (Sir)	ed, ing, ly, -errant, hood, s
knit	ted, ting, ter, s
knitting-needle	s
knob	s
knobbl y	ier, iest, iness
knock	ed, ing, er, -out, s
knot* (tied string; sea speed)	ted, ting, s
knott y	ier, iest, ily, iness
know* (understand)	n, ing, ingly, s
knowledge	able
knuckle	d, øing, -bone, -duster, s

la

label	led, ling, s
laborator y	ies
labour	ed, ing, er, s
lace	d, øing, s
lack	ed, ing, s
lacquer	ed, ing, s
lacrosse	
ladder	ed, ing, s
laden	
lad y	ies
ladybird	s
lag	ged, ging, gard, s
lagoon	s
laid	
lain* (lie flat)	
lair* (den)	s
lake	s
lamb	ed, ing, -chop, kin, skin, swool, s
lame	d, øing, r, st, ly, ness, s
lament	ed, ing, able, ation, s
lamp	light, -post, shade, -standard, s
lance	d, øing, -corporal, r, s

land	ed, ing, mark, scape, slide, slip, s
landlad y	ies
landlord	s
lane* (narrow road)	s
language	s
lantern	s
lap	ped, ping, s
lapel	s
lapse	d, øing, s
larch	es
lard	ed, ing, s
larder	s
large	r, st, ly, ness
lark	s
larva* (insect grub)	e
lash	ed, ing, es
lass	es
lasso	ed, ing, es or s
last	ed, ing, ly, s
latch	ed, ing, es
late	r, st, ly, ness
lathe	s
lather	ed, ing, s
latitude	s
latter	ly
laugh	able, ed, ing, s
laughter	
launch	ed, ing, es
launder	ette, ed, ing, s
laundress	es
laundr y	ies
laurel	s
lava* (volcanic rock)	s
lavator y	ies
lavender	-water
law	ful, less, -breaker, -court, s
lawyer	s

ø Drop e before adding *ing*

*	knight	knot	know		lain	lair	larva
	night	not	no		lane	layer	lava

le   li

lawn	*-mower, -sprinkler, s*
lay	*ing, about, -by, out, er, s*
laid	
layer* (coat; thickness)	*ed, ing, s*
laze	*d, ∉ing, s*
laz *y*	*ier, iest, ily, iness*

le

lead* (metal)	*ed, en, -poisoning, s*
lead (be first)	*ing, er, s*
leaf	*ed, ing, less, -stalk,* **leaves**
leaf *y*	*ier, iest, iness*
leaflet	*s*
league	*s*
leak* (hole; crack)	*age, ed, ing, s*
leak *y*	*ier, iest, iness*
lean	*er, est, ly, ness*
lean	*ed, ing, s*
leant* or **leaned**	
leap	*ed, ing, frog, -year, s*
leapt or **leaped**	
learn	*ed, ing, er, s*
learnt or **learned**	
least	
leather	*y, s*
leave	*∉ing, r, s*
lecture	*d, ∉ing, r, s*
led* (guided)	
ledge	*s*
leek* (vegetable)	*s*
left	
leg	*ged, ging, less, -iron, -rest, s*
legend	*ary, s*
legion	*s*
leisure	*ly*
lemon	*ade, -drop, -juice, -peel, -tree, s*

lend	*ing, er, s*
length	*s*
lengthen	*ed, ing, s*
length *y*	*ier, iest, ily, iness*
lenient	*ly*
lens	*es*
lent* (lend)	
leopard	*skin, s*
leotard	*s*
leper	*s*
leprosy	
less	*er*
lessen* (make smaller)	*ed, ing, s*
lesson* (thing learnt)	*s*
let	*ting, s*
let's (let us)	
letter	*ed, ing, -writer, s*
letter-box	*es*
lettuce	*s*
level	*led, ling, -crossing, s*
lever	*age, ed, ing, s*

li

liable	
liar* (one who lies)	*s*
liberal	*s*
libert *y*	*ies*
librarian	*s*
librar *y*	*ies*
licence* (noun)	*s*
license* (verb)	*d, ∉ing, s*
lick	*ed, ing, er, s*
licorice or **liquorice**	
lie	*d, s*
lying	
lieutenant	*-colonel, -general, s*

∉ Drop **e** before adding *ing*

lo

life	*less, like, line, long, size, time.* **lives**
life	*boat, belt, -guard, -jacket, -saving*
lift	*ed, ing, er, s*
light	*er, est, ly, ness, weight, s*
light	*ed, ing, ish, er, house, ship, s*
lighten	*ed, ing, s*
lightning	*-conductor*
like	*able, d, ∅ing, ness, s*
likel *y*	*ier, iest, ihood*
lilac	*-tree, s*
lil *y*	*ies*
limb	*less, s*
lime	*-juice, light, -tree, s*
limit	*ed, ing, less, s*
limp *ed, ing, er, est, ly, ness, s*	
limpet	*s*
line	*d, ∅ing, sman, smen, s*
linen	*s*
liner	*s*
linger	*ed, ing, er, s*
link	*ed, ing, s*
linoleum or **lino**	*s*
lion	*-tamer, s*
lioness	*es*
lip	*-reading, stick, s*
liquid	*s*
liquorice or **licorice**	
list	*ed, ing, s*
listen	*ed, ing, er, s*
lit or **lighted**	
literature	
litter *ed, ing, -basket, -bin, -bug, -lout, s*	
little	*ness*
live	*d, ∅ing, r, s*
livel *y*	*ier, iest, ily, iness*
liver	*ish, s*
lizard	*s*

lo

load	*ed, ing, er, s*
loaf	**loaves**
loan* (lend)	*ed, ing, s*
loathe	*d, ∅ing, s*
loathsome	*ly, ness*
lob	*bed, bing, ber, s*
lobb *y*	*ies*
lobster	*-pot, s*
local	*ly, s*
localit *y*	*ies*
locate	*d, ∅ing, s*
location	*s*
lock	*ed, ing, er, smith, s*
locket	*s*
locomotive	*s*
locust	*s*
lodge	*d, ∅ing, r, s*
loft	*s*
loft *y*	*ier, iest, ily, iness*
log *ged, ging, -book, -cabin, s*	
loganberr *y*	*ies*
loiter	*ed, ing, er, s*
loll	*ed, ing, er, s*
lollipop	*s*
loll *y*	*ies*
lone* (alone)	*r, some*
lonel *y*	*ier, iest, ily, iness*
long *ed, ing, ingly, er, est, bow, -stop, s*	
longitude	*s*
look	*ed, ing, er, -out, s*
looking-glass	*es*
loom	*ed, ing, s*
loop	*ed, ing, hole, s*
loose	*r, st, ly, ness*
loosen	*ed, ing, s*
loot* (plunder)	*ed, ing, er, s*

∅ Drop **e** before adding *ing*

*	loan	loot
	lone	lute

lu ly ma

lop	ped, ping, -sided, s
lord	ship, s
lorr y	ies
lose	ǿing, r, s
loss	es
lost	
lotion	s
lotto	
loud	er, est, ish, ly, ness, -speaker
lounge	d, ǿing, r, s
lout	ish, s
love	d, ǿing, r, bird, -letter, -song, s
lovel y	ier, iest, ily, iness
low	er, est, ly, ness, s
lower	ed, ing, s
lowland	er, s
loyal	ist, ly, ty
lozenge	s

lu

lubricate	d, ǿing, s
lubrication	
luck	less
luck y	ier, iest, ily, iness
ludo	
lug	ged, ging, s
luggage	-carrier, -rack, -van
lukewarm	ly, ness
lull	ed, ing, s
lullab y	ies
lumbago	s
lumber	ed, ing, er, jack, -room, s
luminous	ly, ness
lump	ed, ing, s
lump y	ier, iest, ily, iness
lunatic	s

lunch	ed, ing, -box, es
luncheon	s
lung	s
lunge	d, ǿing, s
lupin	s
lurch	ed, ing, es
lure	d, ǿing, s
lurk	ed, ing, er, s
luscious	ly, ness
lustr e	ous
lust y	ier, iest, ily, iness
lute* (musical instrument)	s
luxuriant	ly
luxurious	ly, ness
luxur y	ies

ly

lying	
lynch	ed, ing, es
lynx	es or **lynx**
lyre* (musical instrument)	s
lyric	al, s

ma

macaroni	
mace	-bearer, s
machine	d, ǿing, -gun, s
machinery	
machinist	s
mackerel	s or **mackerel**
mackintosh	es
mad	der, dest, ly, ness, house, man, men
madden	ed, ing, s
madam	s
madame (French)	**mesdames**

ǿ Drop **e** before adding *ing*

*	lute	lyre
	loot	liar

made* (make)		**maniac**	s
magazine	s	**manicure**	d, ǿing, s
maggot	y, s	**manner*** (way; behaviour)	ed, s
magic	al, ally	**manoeuvre**	d, ǿing, s
magician	s	**manor*** (lord's land)	-house, s
magistrate	s	**mansion**	s
magnet	ic, ically, ism, s	**mantelpiece**	s
magnetize	d, ǿing, s	**manual**	ly, s
magnificent	ly	**manufacture**	d, ǿing, r, s
magnify	ing	**manure**	d, ǿing, s
magnif ied	ies	**manuscript**	s
magpie	s	**many**	
maid* (girl)	en, servant, s	**map** ped, ping, per, -reading, s	
mail* (armour; post)	ed, ing, -bag, s	**marble**	s
maim	ed, ing, s	**March**	es
main* (chief)	ly, land, stay, s	**march**	ed, ing, es
maintain	ed, ing, s	**mare*** (female horse)	s
maison(n)ette	s	**margarine**	s
maize* (corn)		**margin**	s
majest y	ic, ically, ies	**marigold**	s
major	ette, -general, s	**marine**	r, s
majorit y	ies	**marionette**	s
make ǿing, -believe, shift, -up, r, s		**mark** ed, ing, sman, smen, er, s	
malaria		**market** ed, ing, -day, -place, -stall, s	
male* (man; masculine)	s	**marmalade**	s
mallet	s	**maroon**	ed, ing, s
mammal	s	**marquee**	s
mammoth	s	**marriage**	s
man ned, ning, hole, hood, **men**		**marry**	ing
manl y ier, iest, ily, iness		**marr** ied	ies
manage d, ǿing, able, ably, ment, s		**marrow**	s
manager	s	**Mars**	
manageress	es	**marsh**	es
mandolin	s	**marsh** y	ier, iest, iness
mane* (hair)	s	**marshal**	led, ling, s
manger	s	**marsh-mallow**	s
mangle	d, ǿing, s	**martyr**	ed, ing, dom, s

ǿ Drop ǿ before adding ing

*	made	mail	main	maize	manner	mare
	maid	male	mane	maze	manor	mayor

marvel	led, ling, s
marvellous	ly, ness
marzipan	
mascot	s
masculine	s
mash	ed, ing, es
mask	ed, ing, s
mason	ry, s
masquerade	d, ∉ing, r, s
mass	ed, ing, es
massacre	d, ∉ing, s
massage	d, ∉ing, s
masseur	s
masseuse	s
massive	ly, ness
mast	ed, -head, s
master	ed, ing, ly, y, mind, piece, s
mat	ted, ting, s
matador	s
match	ed, ing, sticks, wood, box, es
mate	d, ∉ing, s
material	s
mathematic	al, ally, ian, s
matinée	s
matron	s
matter	ed, ing, s
mattress	es
maul	ed, ing, s
mauve	r, st, s
maximum	a
may	be
May	s
maypole	s
mayonnaise	
mayor* (head of town or city)	s
mayoress	es
maze* (puzzle)	s

me

meadow	s
meagre	ly, ness
meal	-time, s
mean	er, est, ly, ness, s
meaning	less, s
meant	
meantime	
meanwhile	
measles	
measure	d, ∉ing, ment, s
meat* (flesh)	y, -axe, -ball, -pie, s
mechanic	al, ally, s
mechanism	s
mechanize	d, ∉ing, s
medal* (badge—for bravery, etc.)	s
medallion	s
meddle* (interfere)	d, ∉ing, some, r, s
medi(a)eval	
medical	ly, s
medicine	s
Mediterranean	
medium	s or **media**
meek	er, est, ly, ness
meet* (come together)	ing, s
megaphone	s
melody	ious, iously, ies
melon	s
melt	ed, ing, s
member	ship, s
memorial	s
memorize	d, ∉ing, s
memory	ies
menace	d, ∉ing, s
menagerie	s
mend	ed, ing, er, s
mental	ity, ly

∉ Drop **e** before adding *ing*

* maze	mayor	meat	medal
maize	mare	meet	meddle

mi

mention	*ed, ing, s*
menu	*s*
merchant	*s*
merciful	*ly, ness*
merciless	*ly, ness*
mercy	*ies*
mercury	
mere	*ly*
meringue	*s*
merit	*ed, ing, s*
mermaid	*s*
merry	*ier, iest, ily, iment*
mesmerize	*d, ǿing, s*
mess	*ed, ing, es*
messy	*ier, iest, ily, iness*
message	*s*
messenger	*s*
metal	*lic, work, -detector, s*
meteor	*ic, ite, oid, ology, ologist, s*
meter* (measuring box)	*s*
method	*ical, ically, s*
methylated spirit(s)	
metre* (length measure)	*s*
mew	*ed, ing, s*

mi

miaow	*ed, ing, s*
mice	
microphone	*s*
microscope	*s*
midday	
middle	*-aged, -class*
midge	*s*
midget	*s*
midnight	
midst	
midway	

might	
mighty	*ier, iest, ily, iness*
migrate	*d, ǿing, s*
migration	*s*
mild	*er, est, ly, ness*
mildew	*ed, ǿing, s*
mile	*age, stone, s*
military	
milk	*ed, ing, er, man, men, -shake, s*
milky	*ier, iest, ily, iness*
mill	*ed, ing, er, -pond, stone, s*
millimetre	*s*
million	*th, s*
millionaire	*s*
millionairess	*es*
mime	*d, ǿing, s*
mimic	*ked, king, s*
mince	*d, ǿing, r, meat, -pie, s*
mind*	*ed, ing, er, ful, less, -reader, s*
mine	*d,* ǿing, field, sweeper, s*
miner* (mine worker)	*s*
mineral	*s*
mingle	*d, ǿing, s*
miniature	*s*
minimum	*a*
minister	*s*
minnow	*s*
minor* (young person; lesser)	*s*
minstrel	*s*
mint	*ed, ing, y, -sauce, s*
minus	*es*
minute	*-hand, s*
minute (small)	*ly, ness*
miracle	*s*
miraculous	*ly, ness*
mirage	*s*
mirror	*ed, ing, s*

ǿ Drop **e** before adding *ing*

*	meter		mind	miner
	metre		mined	minor

mo

mirth	
misbehave	d, ∅ing, s
misbehaviour	
mischief	-maker
mischievous	ly, ness
miser	ly, s
miserabl e	y
miser y	ies
misfortune	s
mishap	s
mislay	ing, s
mislaid	
misplace	d, ∅ing, s
miss	ed*, ing, es
missile	s
mission	s
missionar y	ies
mist* (haze; fog)	ed, ing, s
mist y	ier, iest, ily, iness
mistake	n, ∅ing, s
mistook	
mistletoe	
mistress	es
mistrust	ed, ing, s
mitten	s
mix	ed, ing, es
mixer	s
mixture	s

mo

moan* (groan)	ed, ing, er, s
moat	ed, s
mob	bed, bing, s
mobile	s
moccasin	s
mock	ed, ing, s

mocker y	ies
model	led, ling, ler, s
moderate	d, ∅ing, ly, ness, s
modern	ity, ly, ness, s
modernize	d, ∅ing, s
modest	ly, y
moist	ure, ly, ness
moisten	ed, ing, s
mole	hill, skin, s
moment	s
monarch	s
monaster y	ies
Monday	s
money	-lender, -order, -spider, s
mongrel	s
monitor	s
monitress	es
monk	s
monkey	-nut, s
monotonous	ly, ness
monster	s
month	s
monthl y	ies
monument	s
mood	s
mood y	ier, iest, ily, iness
moon	beam, less, light, s
moor	hen, land, s
moor	age, ed, ing, s
mop	ped, ping, per, head, s
moral	ly, s
more	over
morning* (a.m.)	s
morsel	s
mortal	ly, s
mortar	-board, s
mosaic	s

∅ Drop e before adding ing

* missed / mist / moan / mown / morning / mourning

mu   my

mosquito	*es*
moss	*es*
moss *y*	*ier, iest, iness*
most	*ly*
motel	*s*
moth	*-eaten, -proof, ball, s*
mother	*ed, ing, less, ly, hood, s*
motion	*ed, ing, less, -picture, s*
motor	*ed, ing, -bike, -boat, -car, ist, s*
motor	*-cycle, -cyclist, -scooter, way, s*
motto	*es*
mould	*ed, ing, er, s*
mould *y*	*ier, iest, iness*
moult	*ed, ing, s*
mound	*s*
mount	*ed, ing, s*
mountain	*ous, side, -top, s*
mountaineer	*ing, s*
mourn *ing** (sorrowing)	*ed, ful, fully, er, s*
mouse	*d, ǿing, ǿy, r, -hole, trap.* **mice**
moustache	*s*
mouth	*-organ, ful, s*
movable	*s*
move	*d, ǿing, r, ment, s*
mow	*ed, ing, er, s*
mown* (cut grass, etc.)	

mu

much	
mud	*-bank, -bath, -flat, guard*
mudd *y*	*ier, iest, ily, iness*
muddle	*d, ǿing, r, s*
muffle	*d, ǿing, r, s*
mulberr *y*	*ies*
mule	*teer, s*
multiplication	

multiply	*ing*
multipl *ied*	*ier, ies*
multitude	*s*
mumble	*d, ǿing, r, s*
mumm *y*	*ies*
mumps	
munch	*ed, ing, es*
mural	*s*
murder	*ed, ing, er, s*
murderess	*es*
murmur	*ed, ing, er, s*
muscle* (of body)	*s*
museum	*s*
mushroom	*s*
music	*al, ally, -case, -hall, -stand*
musician	*s*
musket	*eer, -shot, s*
mussel* (shellfish)	*s*
must	
mustn't (must not)	
mustard	*-pot*
must *y*	*ier, iest, ily, iness*
mutineer	*s*
mutiny	*ing*
mutin *ied*	*ies*
mutter	*ed, ing, er, s*
mutton	*-chop, -cutlet*
muzzle	*d, ǿing, s*

my

myrrh	
myself	
myster *y*	*ies*
mysterious	*ly, ness*
mystify	*ing*
mystif *ied*	*ies*

ǿ Drop **e** before adding *ing*

★	mourning	mown
	morning	moan

muscle
mussel

na

nail *ed, ing, -scissors, -file, s*
naked *ly, ness*
name *d, ∉ing, ly, less, -plate, sake, s*
nanny *ies*
napkin *-ring, s*
nappy *ies*
narcissus *es* or **narcissi**
narrate *d, ∉ing, s*
narrow *ed, ing, er, est, ish, ly, ness, s*
nasturtium *s*
nasty *ier, iest, ily, iness*
nation *al, ally, wide, s*
nationality *ies*
native *s*
nativity *ies*
natural *ly, ness*
naturalist *s*
nature *s*
naughty *ier, iest, ily, iness*
nautical *ly*
naval
nave* (main part of church) *s*
navigate *d, ∉ing, s*
navigation
navigator *s*
navy *ies*

ne

near *ed, ing, er, est, ly, ness, s*
neat *er, est, ly, ness*
necessary *ily, ies*
necessity *ies*
neck *lace, let, line, tie, s*
need* (want) *ed, ing, s*
needn't (need not)

needle *work, -case, s*
negative *s*
neglect *ed, ing, s*
neglectful *ly, ness*
Negress *es*
Negro *es*
neigh *ed, ing, s*
neighbour *ing, ly, hood, s*
neither
nephew *s*
nerve *d, ∉ing, -racking, s*
nervous *ly, ness*
nest *ed, ing, -egg, ful, s*
nestle *d, ∉ing, s*
net *ted, ting, ball, ful, s*
nettle *s*
neutral *s*
never *more, theless*
new* (just made) *er, est, ly, ness*
news *caster, -letter, -reel, -sheet, y*
newsagent *s*
newspaper *man, men, -boy, -girl, s*
newt *s*
next

ni

nibble *d, ∉ing, r, s*
nice *r, st, ly, ness*
nick *ed, ing, s*
nickname *d, ∉ing, s*
niece *s*
night* *-club, fall, -light, mare, -time, s*
nightingale *s*
nil
nimble *r, st, ness, -footed*
nimbly

*∉ Drop **e** before adding ing*

no

no* (not any; opp. of yes)	*es*
noble	*r, st, man, men, s*
nobody	*ies*
nod	*ded, ding, der, s*
noise	*less, lessly, s*
noisy	*ier, iest, ily, iness*
nomad	*ic, s*
none* (not any)	
nonsense	
noodle	*s*
noon	*day*
noose	*s*
normal	*ly*
Norman	*s*
north	*-east, -west, ern, erly, wards*
nose	*d, ḏing, bag, blced, dive, gay, s*
nostril	*s*
not* (no)	
notable	*s*
notch	*ed, ing, es*
note	*d, ḏing, book, case, paper, let, s*
nothing	
notice	*d, ḏing, able, ably, -board, s*
notify	*ing*
notified	*ication, ies*
notion	*s*
nougat	
nought	*s*
nourish	*ment, ed, ing, es*
novel	*ist, s*
novelty	*ies*
November	*s*
novice	*s*
now	*adays*
nowhere	
nozzle	*s*

nu

nuclear	
nude	*s*
nudist	*s*
nudge	*d, ḏing, s*
nugget	*s*
nuisance	*s*
numb	*ed, ing, ly, ness, s*
number	*ed, ing, -plate, s*
numeral	*s*
numerical	*ly*
numerous	*ly*
nun* (religious woman)	*s*
nurse	*d, ḏing, maid, s*
nursery	*ies*
nut	*ted, ting, cracker, shell, -tree, s*
nutty	*ier, iest, ily, iness*
nuthatch	*es*
nutmeg	*s*
nutrition	*al, ist*
nutritious	*ly, ness*
nuzzle	*d, ḏing, s*

ny

nylon	*s*
nymph	*s*

oa

oaf* (stupid person)	*ish, s* or **oaves**
oak	*-apple, -tree, s*
oar* (rowing blade)	*sman, smen, s*
oasis	*es*
oast	*-house, s*
oat	*meal, cake, s*
oath* (promise; swear-word)	*s*

ḏ Drop **e** before adding *ing*

*	no	none	not	oaf	oar
	know	nun	knot	oath	ore
					or

ob

obedience	
obedient	*ly*
obey	*ed, ing, s*
object	*ed, ing, or, s*
objection	*able, ably, s*
obligation	*s*
oblige	*d, ∉ing, s*
obliterate	*d, ∉ing, s*
oblong	*s*
oboe	*∉ist, s*
obscure	*d, ∉ing, ly, s*
obscurity	
observant	*ly*
observation	*s*
observator *y*	*ies*
observe	*d, ∉ing, r, s*
obstacle	*-course, -race, s*
obstinate	*ly*
obstruct	*ed, ing, ion, s*
obtain	*able, ed, ing, s*
obvious	*ly, ness*

oc

occasion	*al, ally, s*
occupant	*s*
occupation	*s*
occupy	*ing*
occup *ied*	*ier, ies*
occur	*red, ring, rence, s*
ocean	*s*
o'clock	
octagon	*al, s*
October	*s*
octopus	*es* or **octopodes**
oculist	*s*

od

odd	*er, est, ly, ness, ment, s*
odious	*ly, ness*
odour	*s*

of

of	
off	*ing, hand, chance, -side, spring*
offence	*s*
offend	*ed, ing, er, s*
offensive	*ly, ness*
offer	*ed, ing, s*
offertor *y*	*ies*
office	*-block, -boy, -girl, -worker, s*
officer	*s*
official	*ly, s*
often	*er, est*

og

ogre	*s*
ogress	*es*

oi

oil	*ed, ing, can, -rig, -stove, -well, s*
oil	*-heater, -painting, skin, -tanker, s*
oil *y*	*ier, iest, ily, iness*
ointment	*s*

ol

old	*en, er, est, ish, -time*
old-fashioned	*ness*
olive	*-oil, -grove, -tree, s*
Olympic Games or **Olympics**	

*∉ Drop **e** before adding *ing*

om on op   or os ot

om	
omelet(te)	s
omen	s
omission	s
omit	ted, ting, s
omnibus	es

on	
once	
oncoming	
one*	self, -sided, s
onion	y, -skin, s
onlooker	s
only	
onslaught	s
onto	
onward	s

op	
opal	s
opaque	ly, ness
open	ed, ing, ly, ness, er, s
opera	-glasses, -house, -singer, s
operatic	s
operate	d, ∉ing, s
operation	s
operator	s
opinion	s
opponent	s
opportunit y	ies
oppose	d, ∉ing, s
opposite	ly, ness
opposition	
optician	s
optimist	ic, ically, s

or	
oral	ly
orange	ade, -blossom, -peel, -tree, s
orang-(o)utan	s
orator	s
orbit	ed, ing, s
orchard	s
orchestra	l, s
orchid	s
ordeal	s
order	ed, ing, s
orderl y	iness, ies
ordinar y	ily, iness
ore* (metal in rock)	s
organ	-grinder, -loft, -pipe, ist, s
organization	s
organize	d, ∉ing, r, s
orient	
oriental	s
origin	s
original	ity, ly
originate	d, ∉ing, s
ornament	ed, ing, al, ation, s
ornithologist	s
ornithology	
orphan	ed, ing, age, s

os	
osier	s
ostrich	es

ot	
other	s
otherwise	
otter	s

∉ Drop **e** before adding *ing*

*	one (1)	ore
	won	oar
		or

ou   ov   ow   ox   oy

ou	
ought	
ounce	s
our* (belonging to us)	s
ourselves	
out	come, let, look, put, right, standing
outbreak	s
outburst	s
outcast	s
outer	most
outfit	ted, ting, ter, s
outhouse	s
outing	s
outlaw	ed, ing, s
outline	d, ǿing, s
outnumber	ed, ing, s
out-patient	s
outpost	s
outrage	d, ǿing, s
outrageous	ly, ness
outside	r, s
outskirts	
outward	ly, ness, s
outwit	ted, ting, s

ov	
oval	s
oven	s
over	s
overall	s
overbalance	d, ǿing, s
overboard	
overcame	
overcome	ǿing, s
overcoat	s
overcrowd	ed, ing, s

overdose	d, ǿing, s
overflow	ed, ing, s
overhaul	ed, ing, s
overhead	s
overhear	ing, s
overheard	
overjoyed	
overlap	ped, ping, s
overload	ed, ing, s
overlook	ed, ing, s
overpower	ed, ing, s
overseas	
oversleep	ing, s
overslept	
overtake	n, ǿing, s
overtook	
overthrow	n, ing, s
overthrew	
overtime	
overturn	ed, ing, s
overwhelm	ed, ing, s
overwork	ed, ing, s

ow	
owe	d, ǿing, s
owl	et, s
own	ed, ing, er, s

ox	
ox	en
oxlip	s
oxygen	

oy	
oyster	-bed, -catcher, -farm, -shell, s

ǿ Drop **e** before adding *ing*.

*   our
    hour

pa

pa	
pace	d, ∅ing, r, s
Pacific	
pack	ed, ing, er, s
package	d, ∅ing, s
packet	ed, ing, s
pad	ded, ding, der, s
paddle	d, ∅ing, r, -boat, -steamer, s
padlock	ed, ing, s
page	-boy, s
pageant	s
paid	
pail* (bucket)	ful, s
pain* (suffering)	ed, ing, -killer, s
painful	ly, ness
painless	ly, ness
paint	ed, ing, er, s
pair* (two)	ed, ing, s
palace	s
pale* (faint; whitish)	r, st, ly, ness, s
palette	s
palm	-tree, s
pamper	ed, ing, er, s
pamphlet	s
pan	ned, ning, ful, cake, s
panda	s
pane* (sheet of glass)	s
panel	led, ling, list, s
panic	ked, king, ky, -stricken, -struck, s
panorama	s
pansy	ies
pant	ed, ing, s
panther	s
pantomime	s
pantry	ies
paper	ed, ing, -boy, -girl, -chain, -clip, s
papier mâché	

parachute	d, ∅ing, -troops, s
parade	d, ∅ing, -ground, s
paraffin	-heater, -oil
parallel	ed, ing, s
paralyse	d, ∅ing, s
paralysis	es
paratroops	
parcel	led, ling, s
parch	ed, ing, es
parchment	s
pardon	able, ed, ing, s
pare* (cut away; peel)	d, ∅ing, s
parent	age, al, s
parish	es
park	ed, ing, land, -keeper, s
parliament	s
parrot	s
parsley	-sauce
parsnip	s
parson	age, s
part	ed, ing, ly, s
particle	s
particular	ly, s
partition	ed, ing, s
partner	ed, ing, ship, s
partridge	s
party	ies
pass	ed*, ing, able, es
passage	way, s
passenger	s
passion	ate, ately, s
passport	s
password	s
past* (time gone by)	
paste	d, ∅ing, s
pastel* (crayon)	led, ling, s
pastille* (sweet)	s

∅ Drop e before adding *ing*

*	pail	pain	pair		passed	pastel
	pale	pane	pare		past	pastille
			pear			

pe

pastime	s
pastr y	ies
pasture	d, ∉ing, s
past y	ies
pat	ted, ting, s
patch	ed, ing, work, es
patch y	ier, iest, ily, iness
path	way, s
pathetic	ally
patience	
patient	ly, s
patrol	led, ling, man, men, -leader, s
patter	ed, ing, s
pattern	ed, ing, -book, s
pause* (hesitate)	d, ∉ing, s
pave	d, ∉ing, ment, s
pavilion	s
paw (animal's foot)	s,* ed, ing
pawn	ed, ing, broker, shop, -ticket, s
pay	able, ing, er, ment, -day, -desk, s
paid	

pe

pea	nut, -pod, -soup, -shooter, s
peace* (quiet)	able, -offering, -time
peaceful	ly, ness
peach	es
peacock	s
peahen	s
peak	ed, ing, s
peal* (sound of bells)	ed, ing, s
pear* (fruit)	-drop, -tree, s
pearl	-diver, -fisher, s
peasant	ry, s
peat	-bog, -moor, y
pebble	-stone, s
pebbl y	ier, iest, iness

peck	ed, ing, er, s
peculiar	ly
peculiarit y	ies
pedal* (foot-lever)	led, ling, -cycle, s
peddle* (to hawk goods)	d, ∉ing, s
pedestrian	s
pedigree	s
pedlar	s
peel* (skin of fruit)	ed, ing, er, s
peep	ed, ing, er, -hole, -show, s
peer* (stare)	ed, ing, s
peg	ged, ging, s
Pekin(g)ese	**Pekin(g)ese**
pelican	s
pellet	s
pelt	ed, ing, s
pen	ned, ning, -friend, -nib, s
penalt y	ies
pence	
pencil	led, ling, -case, -sharpener, s
pendulum	s
penetrate	d, ∉ing, s
penguin	s
peninsula	s
pen knife	knives
pennant	s
penn y	ies or **pence**
penniless	ly, ness
pension	ed, ing, able, er, -book, s
people	s
pepper	ed, ing, y, -pot, mint, s
perambulator	s
perch	ed, ing, es
percussion	-band, s
perfect	ly, ed, ing, ion, s
perform	ed, ing, ance, er, s
perfume	d, ∉ing, s

∉ Drop **e** before adding *ing*

*	pause	peace	pear	peal	pedal	peer
	paws	piece	pair	peel	peddle	pier
			pare			

ph

perhaps	
peril	*ous, ously, s*
period	*ic, ical, ically, s*
periscope	*s*
perish	*ed, ing, es*
permanent	*ly*
permission	
permit	*ted, ting, s*
perplex	*ed, ing, es*
persevere	*d, ǿing, ǿance, s*
persist	*ed, ing, ence, ent, s*
person	*al, ally, s*
perspiration	
perspire	*d, ǿing, s*
persuade	*d, ǿing, s*
persuasion	
persuasive	*ly, ness*
pessimist	*ic, ically, s*
pester	*ed, ing, s*
pet	*ted, ting, -shop, s*
petal	*s*
petrol	*eum, -pump, -station, s*
petticoat	*s*
pew	*s*
pewter	

ph

phantom	*s*
pheasant	*s*
philatelist	*s*
phone	*d, ǿing. -booth, s*
photo	*-fit, -frame, s*
photograph	*ed, ing, y, er, s*
physical	*ly*
physician	*s*
physics	

*ǿ Drop **e** before adding ing*

pi

pi

pi* ($\pi = 3.14159$)	
pianist	*s*
piano	*-accordion, -stool, s*
piccolo	*-player, s*
pick	*ed, ing, er, axe, pocket, s*
pickle	*d, ǿing, r, s*
picnic	*ked, king, ker, -basket, s*
picture	*d, ǿing, -book, -frame, s*
picturesque	*ly, ness*
pie*	*crust, -shop, s*
piece* (a part)	*d, ǿing, s*
pier* (jetty)	*s*
pierce	*d, ǿing, s*
pierrot	*s*
pig	*let, skin, s*
pigst *y*	*ies*
pigeon	*-hole, -house, -loft, s*
pigm *y* or **pygm** *y*	*ies*
pigtail	*s*
pike	*man, men, staff, s*
pilchard	*s*
pile	*d, ǿing, s*
pilgrim	*age, s*
pillar	*s*
pillar-box	*es*
pillion	*-rider, -seat, s*
pillow	*case, slip, -fight, s*
pilot	*ed, ing, s*
pimple	*d, ǿing, s*
pimpl *y*	*ier, iest, iness*
pin	*ned, ning, cushion, s*
pincers	**pincers**
pinch	*ed, ing, es*
pine	*d, ǿing, apple, -cone, -needle, -tree, s*
pink	*er, est, ish, y, ness, s*
pint	*s*

*	pi	piece	pier
	pie	peace	peer

pl

pioneer	*ed, ing, s*
pipe	*d, ₫ing, r, -cleaner, ful, s*
piranha	*s*
pirate	*s*
pistil* (part of flower)	*s*
pistol* (small gun)	*-shot, s*
pit	*ted, ting, fall, -head, -prop, s*
pitch	*ed, ing, -black, -dark, es*
pitchfork	*ed, ing, s*
piteous	*ly*
pity	*ing*
pit *ied*	*iful, iless, ies*
pixie	*s or* **pix** *y, ies*
pizza	*s*

pl

placard	*s*
place* (position)	*d, ing, s*
plague	*d, ₫ing, s*
plaice* (fish)	**plaice**
plain*	*er, est, ly, ness, s*
plait	*ed, ing, s*
plan	*ned, ning, ner, s*
plane* (tool; to smooth)	*d, ₫ing, s*
plane* (aeroplane; tree)	*s*
planet	*s*
plank	*ed, ing, s*
plant	*ed, ing, ation, er, s*
plaster	*ed, ing, er, s*
plastic	*s*
plasticine	
plate	*d, ₫ing, ful, -glass, -rack, s*
platform	*s*
platinum	
play	*ed, ing, ground, mate, time, er, s*
play	*-group, -pen, thing, wright, s*
playful	*ly, ness*

po

plead	*ed, ing, s*
pleasant	*ly, ness*
please	*d, ₫ing, s*
pleasure	*s*
pleat	*ed, ing, s*
plentiful	*ly, ness*
plenty	
pliers	**pliers**
plimsoll	*s*
plod	*ded, ding, der, s*
plot	*ted, ting, ter, s*
plough	*ed, ing, man, men, boy, s*
pluck	*ed, ing, er, s*
pluck *y*	*ier, iest, ily, iness*
plug	*ged, ging, ger, s*
plum*	*-pudding, -stone, -tree, s*
plumage	
plumb*	*ed, ing, -line, s*
plumber	*s*
plump	*er, est, ly, ness*
plunder	*ed, ing, er, s*
plunge	*d, ₫ing, r, s*
plural	*s*
plus	*es*

po

poach	*ed, ing, es*
poacher	*s*
pocket	*ed, ing, -book, -money, ful, s*
pocket-*knife*	*-knives*
podg *y*	*ier, iest, ily, iness*
poem	*s*
poet	*ic, ical, ically, s*
poetry	
point	*ed, ing, -blank, -duty, less, er,'s*
poise	*d, ₫ing, s*
poison	*ed, ing, ous, ously, er, s*

₫ Drop e before adding ing

*	pistil	place	plain	plum
	pistol	plaice	plane	plumb

poke	*d, ǿing, r, s*	**portable**	*s*
polar bear	*s*	**porter**	*s*
pole* (long rod)	*-jump, -vault, s*	**porthole**	*s*
police	*d, ǿing, -officer, man, woman*	**portion**	*ed, ing, s*
police force	*s*	**portrait**	*s*
police station	*s*	**pose**	*d, ǿing, s*
polish	*ed, ing, es*	**position**	*ed, ing, s*
polite	*r, st, ly, ness*	**positive**	*ly, ness*
political	*ly*	**possess**	*ed, ing, ive, es*
politician	*s*	**possession**	*s*
poll* (vote)	*ed, ing, s*	**possibilit**y	*ies*
pollen		**possible**	*s*
polo	*-stick*	**possibly**	
polytechnic	*s*	**post**	*ed, ing, man, men, card, mark, s*
polythene		**postage**	*-stamp*
pomp	*ous, ously, osity*	**postal order**	*s*
pond	*-life, -snail, weed, s*	**poster**	*s*
ponder	*ed, ing, s*	**post office**	*s*
pontoon	*-bridge, s*	**postpone**	*d, ǿing, ment, s*
pony	*ies*	**pos**y	*ies*
poodle	*s*	**pot**	*ted, ting, ful, -luck, -hole, -shot, s*
pool	*ed, ing, s*	**potato**	*es*
poor* (not rich)	*er, est, ly, ness*	**potion**	*s*
pop	*ped, ping, per, corn, gun, s*	**potter**	*ed, ing, s*
pop	*-group, -music, -singer, -song, s*	**potter**y	*ies*
poplar	*-tree, s*	**pouch**	*es*
poppy	*ies*	**poultice**	*d, ǿing, s*
popular	*ity, ly*	**poultry**	*-farm*
population		**pounce**	*d, ǿing, s*
porcelain		**pound**	*ed, ing, s*
porch	*es*	**pour*** (flow out)	*ed, ing, er, s*
porcupine	*s*	**pout**	*ed, ing, er, s*
pore* (study; tiny hole)	*d, ǿing, s*	**poverty**	*-stricken*
pork	*-butcher, -chop, -pie, er, y*	**powder**	*ed, ing, y, -puff, -room, s*
porpoise	*s*	**power**	*ed, -house, -plant, -station, s*
porridge		**powerful**	*ly, ness*
port	*s*	**powerless**	*ly, ness*

ǿ Drop **e** before adding *ing*

*	pole	poor
	poll	pore
		pour

pr_a pre   pri   pro

pr	
practical	ly, ity, ness
practice* (noun)	s
practise* (verb)	d, ǿing, s
prairie	s
praise	d, ǿing, s
prance	d, ǿing, s
prank	ster, s
prawn	ed, ing, er, s
pray* (ask God)	ed, ing, s
prayer	-book, -meeting, s
preach	ed, ing, es
preacher	s
precaution	ary, s
precious	ly, ness
precipice	s
prefect	s
prefer	red, ring, able, ably, ence, s
prehistoric	al, ally
preliminary	ies
premises	
preparation	s
prepare	d, ǿing, s
prescribe	d, ǿing, s
prescription	s
presence	
present	ed, ing, ation, s
presently	
preserve	d, ǿing, s
president	s
press	ed, ing, es
pressure	-cooker, -gauge, s
pretend	ed, ing, er, s
pretty	ier, iest, ily, iness
prevent	ed, ing, ion, s
previous	ly, ness
prey* (victim; thing hunted)	ed, ing, s

price	d, ǿing, less, -list, -tag, s
prick	ed, ing, er, s
prickle	d, ǿing, s
prickly	ier, iest, iness
pride* (proudness)	d, ǿing, s
pried* (looked into)	
priest	ly, hood, s
priestess	es
primary school	s
primitive	ly, ness
primrose	s
prince	ly, s
princess	es
principal* (head; chief)	ly, s
principle* (rule; truth)	s
print	ed, ing, er, s
prison	er, s
private	ly, s
privilege	d, ǿing, s
prize	d, ǿing, -winner, s
probability	ies
probable	s
probably	
problem	s
procedure	s
proceed	ed, ing, s
process	ed, ing, es
procession	s
proclaim	ed, ing, s
procure	d, ǿing, s
prod	ded, ding, s
produce	d, ǿing, r, s
product	ive, ion, s
profession	al, ally, s
professor	s
profit* (gain)	able, ed, ing, eer, s
programme	d, ǿing, r, s

ǿ Drop **e** before adding *ing*

*	practice	pray		pride	principal	profit
	practise	prey		pried	principle	prophet

progress	*ed, ing, es*		
prohibit	*ed, ing, s*		**pu**
project	*ed, ing, ile, ion, or, s*	**public**	*ly, -house*
promenade	*d, ∅ing, r, s*	**publication**	*s*
prominent	*ly*	**publicity**	
promise	*d, ∅ing, s*	**publish**	*ed, ing, es*
promote	*d, ∅ing, r, s*	**publisher**	*s*
promotion	*s*	**pudding**	*s*
prompt	*ed, ing, er, est, ly, ness, s*	**puddle**	*s*
pronounce	*d, ∅ing, ment, s*	**puff**	*ed, ing, er, s*
proof	*s*	**puff** *y*	*ier, iest, ily, iness*
prop	*ped, ping, s*	**pull**	*ed, ing, er, s*
propel	*led, ling, ler, s*	**pullover**	*s*
proper	*ly*	**pulley**	*-block, s*
propert *y*	*ies*	**pulp**	*ed, ing, er, s*
prophec *y* (noun)	*ies*	**pulpit**	*s*
prophes *y* (verb)	*ied, ies*	**pulse**	*d, ∅ing, s*
prophesying		**pump**	*ed, ing, s*
prophet* (foreteller of future) *s*		**pumpkin**	*s*
proposal	*s*	**punch**	*ed, ing, es*
propose	*d, ∅ing, r, s*	**punctual**	*ity, ly*
proprietor	*s*	**puncture**	*d, ∅ing, s*
prosecute	*d, ∅ing, s*	**punish**	*able, ed, ing, es*
prosper	*ed, ing, ous, ously, ity, s*	**punishment**	*s*
protect	*ed, ing, ion, ive, or, s*	**punt**	*ed, ing, er, s*
protest	*ed, ing, s*	**pupa**	*e*
Protestant	*s*	**pupil**	*s*
protrude	*d, ∅ing, s*	**puppet**	*ry, -play, -show, s*
proud	*er, est, ly*	**pupp** *y*	*ies*
prove	*d, ∅ing, s*	**purchase**	*d, ∅ing, r, s*
proverb	*s*	**pure**	*r, st, ly, ness*
provide	*d, ∅ing, r, s*	**purity**	
provision	*ed, ing, s*	**purple**	*r, st, ness, s*
prowl	*ed, ing, er, s*	**purpose**	*ly, s*
prune	*d, ∅ing, s*	**purr**	*ed, ing, s*
pry	*ing*	**purse**	*r, -snatcher, s*
pr *ied***	*ies*	**pursue**	*d, ∅ing, r, s*
		pursuit	*s*

∅ Drop **e** before adding *ing*

*	prophet	pried
	profit	pride

push	ed, ing, es
puss y	ies
put	ting, s
putt (golf)	ed, ing, er, s
putting-green	s
putty	
puzzle	d, ⌀ing, r, ment, s

py

pygm y or **pigm** y	ies
pyjamas	
pylon	s
pyramid	s
python	s

qua

quack	ed, ing, s
quadrangle	s
quadruplet	s
quaint	er, est, ly, ness
quake	d, ⌀ing, s
qualification	s
qualify	ing
qualif ied	ies
qualit y	ies
quantit y	ies
quarantine	d, ⌀ing, s
quarrel	led, ling, ler, some, s
quarry	ing
quarr ied	ies
quart (two pints)	s*
quarter	ed, ing, s
quartet(te)	s
quartz* (rock-crystal)	
quay* (wharf)	side, s

que

queen	s
queer	er, est, ly, ness
quell	ed, ing, s
quench	ed, ing, es
query	ing
quer ied	ies
quest	ed, ing, s
question	ed, ing, er, -master, s
queue* (line of persons, etc.)	d, r, s
queueing or **queuing**	

qui

quibble	d, ⌀ing, r, s
quick	er, est, ly, ness
quicken	ed, ing, s
quiet	ed, ing, er, est, ly, ness, s
quieten	ed, ing, s
quill	s
quilt	ed, ing, s
quince	s
quinine	
quintet(te)	s
quintuplet	s
quire* (measure of paper)	s
quit	ted, ting, ter, s
quite	
quiver	ed, ing, s
quiz	zed, zing, zes

quo

quoit	s
quota	s
quotation	-mark, s
quote	d, ⌀ing, s

⌀ Drop **e** before adding *ing*

*	quarts	quay	queue	quire
	quartz	key	cue	choir

ra   rea

ra	
rabbit	*ed, ing, er, -hole, -warren, s*
race	*d, øing, r, course, horse, track, s*
rack	*ed, ing, s*
racket* (noise)	*ed, ing, eer, s*
racket* or **racquet*** (bat)	*s*
radar	
radiate	*d, øing, s*
radiator	*s*
radio	*ed, ing, s*
radish	*es*
radius	*i*
raffle	*d, øing, r, -ticket, s*
raft	*s*
rafter	*s*
rag	*ged, ging, s*
ragged	*ly, ness*
rage	*d, øing, s*
raid	*ed, ing, er, s*
rail	*ing, s*
railway	*-carriage, -crossing, -line, s*
rain*	*ed, ing, -water, bow, coat, drop, s*
rainy	*ier, iest, ily, iness*
raise* (lift up)	*d, øing, s*
raisin	*s*
rake	*d, øing, r, s*
rally	*ing*
rallied	*ies*
ram	*med, ming, rod, s*
ramble	*d, øing, r, s*
ramshackle	
ranch	*es*
rancher	*s*
random	*ly*
rang	
range	*d, øing, r, s*
rank	*ed, ing, s*

re	
ransack	*ed, ing, er, s*
ransom	*ed, ing, s*
rap* (knock)	*ped, ping, s*
rapid	*ity, ly, s*
rare	*r, st, ly, ness*
rascal	*ly, s*
rash	*er, est, ly, ness*
rasher	*s*
raspberry	*ies*
rat	*ted, ting, -hole, -poison, -trap, s*
rate	*d, øing, payer, s*
rather	
ration	*ed, ing, s*
rattle	*d, øing, r, snake, s*
rave	*d, øing, s*
raven	*s*
ravenous	*ly, ness*
ravine	*s*
raw	*er, est, ly, ness*
ray (beam of light)	*s**
razor	*-blade, -edge, -shell, s*

re	
reach	*ed, ing, es*
react	*ed, ing, ion, or, s*
read*	*ing, er, s*
ready	*ier, iest, ily, iness*
real* (true)	*ly, ist, istic, ism*
reality	*ies*
realize	*d, øing, s*
really	
reap	*ed, ing, er, s*
reappear	*ed, ing, ance, s*
rear	*ed, ing, guard, -lamp, -light, ward, s*
rearrange	*d, øing, ment, s*
reason	*ed, ing, able, ably, s*

ø Drop **e** before adding *ing*

*	racket	rain	raise	rap	read	read	real
	racquet	reign	rays	wrap	reed	red	reel
		rein					

reb　rec　red　ree　　ref　reg　reh　rei　rej　rel

rebel	*led, ling, s*	**refer**	*red, ring, s*
rebellion	*s*	**referee**	*d, ing, s*
rebellious	*ly, ness*	**reference**	*-book, s*
rebound	*ed, ing, s*	**reflect**	*ed, ing, ion, or, s*
recall	*ed, ing, s*	**refrain**	*ed, ing, s*
recapture	*d, ¢ing, s*	**refresh**	*ed, ing, es*
receipt	*ed, ing, -book, s*	**refreshment**	*s*
receive	*d, ¢ing, r, s*	**refrigerator**	*s*
recent	*ly, ness*	**refuge**	*s*
receptacle	*s*	**refugee**	*s*
reception	*ist, s*	**refund**	*ed, ing, s*
recess	*ed, ing, es*	**refusal**	*s*
recipe	*s*	**refuse**	*d, ¢ing, s*
recital	*s*	**regain**	*ed, ing, s*
recitation	*s*	**regard**	*ed, ing, less, lessly, s*
recite	*d, ¢ing, s*	**regatta**	*s*
reckless	*ly, ness*	**regiment**	*ed, ing, al, s*
reckon	*ed, ing, er, s*	**region**	*al, s*
recognize	*d, ¢ing, s*	**register**	*ed, ing, s*
recollect	*ed, ing, ion, s*	**regret**	*ted, ting, table, tably, s*
recommend	*ed, ing, ation, s*	**regretful**	*ly*
record	*ed, ing, -player, s*	**regular**	*ity, ly*
recorder	*s*	**regulate**	*d, ¢ing, s*
recover	*ed, ing, s*	**regulation**	*s*
recovery	*ies*	**rehearsal**	*s*
recreation	*-ground, s*	**rehearse**	*d, ¢ing, s*
recruit	*ed, ing, ment, s*	**reign*** (rule)	*ed, ing, s*
rectangle	*s*	**rein*** (strap)	*ed, ing, s*
red* (colour)	*der, dest, dish, dy, ness, s*	**reindeer**	**reindeer**
redden	*ed, ing, s*	**reinforce**	*d, ¢ing, ment, s*
redskin	*s*	**reject**	*ed, ing, ion, s*
redecorate	*d, ¢ing, s*	**rejoice**	*d, ¢ing, s*
reduce	*d, ¢ing, s*	**rejoin**	*ed, ing, s*
reduction	*s*	**relate**	*d, ¢ing, s*
reed* (tall grass)	*s*	**relation**	*s*
reef	*-knot, s*	**relative**	*s*
reel* (spool; dance; stagger)	*ed, ing, s*	**relax**	*ed, ing, es*

*¢ Drop **e** before adding* ing

*	red	reed	reel	reign
	read	read	real	rein
				rain

76

relay	*ed, ing, -race, s*		**request**	*ed, ing, s*
release	*d, øing, s*		**require**	*d, øing, ment, s*
reliable	*ness*		**rescue**	*d, øing, r, s*
relic	*s*		**resemblance**	*s*
relief			**resemble**	*d, øing, s*
relieve	*d, øing, s*		**reservation**	*s*
religion	*s*		**reserve**	*d, øing, s*
religious	*ly, ness*		**reservoir**	*s*
rely	*ing*		**reside**	*d, øing, nce, nt, s*
relied	*iable, ies*		**resign**	*ed, ing, ation, s*
remain	*ed, ing, der, s*		**resist**	*ed, ing, ance, s*
remark	*ed, ing, able, ably, s*		**resolution**	*s*
remedy	*ies*		**resort**	*ed, ing, s*
remember	*ed, ing, s*		**respect**	*ed, ing, able, ably, ful, fully, s*
remembrance	*s*		**responsibilit**y	*ies*
remind	*ed, ing, er, s*		**responsible**	
remnant	*s*		**rest**	*ed, ing, -cure, -home, -room, s*
remote	*ly, ness*		**restful**	*ly, ness*
removal	*s*		**restless**	*ly, ness*
remove	*d, øing, r, s*		**restaurant**	*s*
renew	*ed, ing, able, al, s*		**result**	*ed, ing, s*
rent	*ed, ing, able, al, s*		**resume**	*d, øing, s*
repair	*ed, ing, able, er, s*		**retire**	*d, øing, ment, s*
repay	*ing, able, ment, s*		**retrace**	*d, øing, s*
repaid			**retreat**	*ed, ing, s*
repeat	*ed, edly, ing, er, s*		**retrieve**	*d, øing, r, s*
repetition	*s*		**return**	*ed, ing, able, -ticket, s*
replace	*d, øing, able, ment, s*		**reveal**	*ed, ing, s*
replay	*ed, ing, s*		**revenge**	*d, øing, s*
reply	*ing*		**reverse**	*d, øing, s*
replied	*ies*		**review**	*ed, ing, s*
report	*ed, ing, er, s*		**revive**	*d, øing, s*
represent	*ed, ing, ative, s*		**revolt**	*ed, ing, s*
reproduce	*d, øing, s*		**revolution**	*s*
reptile	*s*		**revolve**	*d, øing, s*
republic	*an, s*		**revolver**	*s*
reputation	*s*		**reward**	*ed, ing, s*

ø Drop **e** before adding *ing*

rh

rheumatism	
rhinoceros	*es*
rhododendron	*s*
rhubarb	
rhyme	*d, e̸ing, s*
rhythm	*ic, ical, ically, s*

ri

rib	*bed, bing, s*
ribbon	*s*
rice	*-pudding, -field, s*
rich	*er, est, ly, ness, es*
rick	*ed, ing, s*
ricket *y*	*iness*
ridden	
riddle	*d, e̸ing, r, s*
ride	*e̸ing, r, s*
riding	*-crop, -school, -stable, -whip, s*
ridge	*s*
ridicule	*d, e̸ing, s*
ridiculous	*ly, ness*
rifle	*d, e̸ing, man, men, -range, -shot, s*
rig	*ged, ging, ger, s*
right* (true; opp. left)	*ful, ly, -handed, s*
rigid	*ity, ly, ness*
rim	*med, ming, less, s*
rind	*s*
ring* (circle)	*ed, ing, leader, -master, s*
ring* (bell sound)	*ing, er, s*
rink	*s*
rinse	*d, e̸ing, r, s*
riot	*ed, ing, er, s*
rip	*ped, ping, per, -cord, s*
ripe	*r, st, ly, ness*
ripen	*ed, ing, s*

ripple	*d, e̸ing, s*
rise	*e̸ing, r, s*
risen	
risk	*ed, ing, s*
risk *y*	*ier, iest, ily, iness*
rissole	*s*
rival	*led, ling, s*
rivalr *y*	*ies*
river	*-bank, -bed, -boat, side, s*
rivet	*ed, ing, er, s*

ro

road* (highway)	*side, way, -sweeper, s*
roam	*ed, ing, er, s*
roar	*ed, ing, er, s*
roast	*ed, ing, er, s*
rob	*bed, bing, ber, s*
robber *y*	*ies*
robe	*d, e̸ing, s*
robin	*-redbreast, s*
robot	*s*
rock	*ed, ing, -cake, -garden, s*
rock *y*	*ier, iest, ily, iness*
rocker *y*	*ies*
rocket	*ed, ing, s*
rode* (ride)	
rodeo	*s*
roe* (deer; fish eggs)	*s*
rogue	*s*
rôle* (actor's part)	*s*
roll* (turn over)	*ed, ing, -call, mop, er, s*
roller-skate	*d, e̸ing, r, s*
Roman	*s*
romance	*d, e̸ing, s*
romantic	*ally, s*
romp	*ed, ing, er, s*

*e̸ Drop **e** before adding ing*

*	right	ring	road	roe	rôle
	write	wring	rode	row	roll
			rowed		

ru

sa

roof	-garden, -rack, -top, s
rook	s
rooker y	ies
room	ful, s
room y	ier, iest, ily, iness
root* (part of a plant)	ed, ing, s
rope	d, ₵ing, -ladder, s
rose	-bud, -garden, -hip, -tree, wood, s
rosette	s
ros y	ier, iest, ily, iness
rot	ted, ting, s
rotate	d, ₵ing, s
rotten	ly, ness
rough	ed, ing, er, est, ly, ness, s
roughen	ed, ing, s
round	ed, ing, ish, ness, sman, smen, s
roundabout	s
rounders	
rouse	d, ₵ing, s
route* (a way)	d, ₵ing, s
routine	s
rove	d, ₵ing, r, s
row (quarrel)	ed, ing, s
row* (line; use oars)	ed,* ing, er, -boat, s
rowing-boat	s
rowd y	ier, iest, ily, iness, ies
royal	ist, ly, ty

ru

rub	bed, bing, s
rubber	-stamp, -tree, s
rubbish	-tip, -heap, y
rubble	
rub y	ies
rucksack	s
rudder	s

rude	r, st, ly, ness
ruffian	s
ruffle	d, ₵ing, s
Rugby	-ball
rugged	ly, ness
ruin	ed, ing, ous, s
rule	d, ₵ing, r, s
rumble	d, ₵ing, s
rummage	d, ₵ing, -sale, s
rumour	ed, ing, s
run	ning, ner, way, s
rung* (ring; ladder step)	s
rural	ly, ness
rush	ed, ing, es
rust	ed, ing, less, -proof, s
rust y	ier, iest, ily, iness
rustle	d, ₵ing, r, s
rut	ted, ting, s
rutt y	ier, iest, iness

sa

sabbath	s
sack	ed, ing, ful, -race, s
sacred	ly, ness
sacrifice	d, ₵ing, s
sad	der, dest, ly, ness
sadden	ed, ing, s
saddle	d, ₵ing, r, -bag, s
safari	s
safe	r, st, ly, ness, s
safety	-catch, -lamp, -net, -pin, -valve
sag	ged, ging, s
sago	s
said	
sail* (travel by ship)	ed, ing, s
sailor	s

₵ Drop **e** before adding *ing*

*	root	row	rowed	rung	sail
	route	roe	road	wrung	sale
			rode		

SC

saint	*s*	**sauce**	*pan, s*
saintl *y*	*ier, iest, ily, iness*	**saucer**	*ful, s*
sake	*s*	**sauc** *y*	*ier, iest, ily, iness*
salad	*-dressing, -oil, s*	**saunter**	*ed, ing, s*
salar *y*	*ies*	**sausage**	*-meat, -roll, s*
sale* (selling)	*sman, smen, -room, s*	**savage**	*d, ∅ing, ly, ry, ness, s*
salmon	**salmon**	**save**	*d, ∅ing, s*
saloon	*s*	**saviour**	*s*
salt	*ed, ing, -water, -cellar, -spoon, s*	**saw**	*ed, ing, dust, mill, s*
salt *y*	*ier, iest, iness*	**sawn** or **sawed**	
salute	*d, ∅ing, s*	**Saxon**	*s*
salvage	*d, ∅ing, s*	**saxophone**	*s*
same	*ness*	**say**	*ing, s*
sample	*d, ∅ing, r, s*	**said**	
sanatorium	*s* or **sanatoria**		
sanctuar *y*	*ies*		
sand	*-castle, -dune, paper, -storm, s*	**sc**	
sand *y*	*ier, iest, iness*	**scabbard**	*s*
sandal	*s*	**scaffold**	*ing, s*
sandwich	*ed, ing, es*	**scald**	*ed, ing, s*
sang		**scale**	*d, ∅ing, s*
sank		**scalp**	*ed, ing, s*
Santa Claus		**scamp**	*ed, ing, s*
sap	*ped, ping, ling, s*	**scamper**	*ed, ing, s*
sapphire	*s*	**scan**	*ned, ning, ner, s*
sarcastic	*ally*	**scar**	*red, ring, s*
sardine	*s*	**scarce**	*r, st, ly, ness*
sash	*es*	**scarcit** *y*	*ies*
satchel	*s*	**scare**	*d, ∅ing, r, crow, s*
satellite	*s*	**scarf**	*-ring, s* or **scarves**
satin	*s*	**scarlet**	*s*
satisfaction		**scatter**	*ed, ing, -brain, s*
satisfactor *y*	*ily, iness*	**scavenge**	*d, ∅ing, r, s*
satisfy	*ing*	**scene*** (view; place)	*-shifter, s*
satisf *ied*	*ies*	**scenery**	
saturate	*d, ∅ing, s*	**scent*** (smell; perfume)	*ed, ing, s*
Saturday	*s*	**scheme**	*d, ∅ing, r, s*

*∅ Drop **e** before adding *ing*

*	sale	scene	scent
	sail	seen	sent

se

scholar	*ship, s*
scholastic	*ally*
school	*ed, ing, boy, girl, -teacher, s*
schoolmaster	*s*
schoolmistress	*es*
schooner	*s*
science	*-fiction, s*
scientific	*ally*
scientist	*s*
scissors	**scissors**
scold	*ed, ing, er, s*
scone	*s*
scoop	*ed, ing, er, s*
scooter	*s*
scorch	*ed, ing, es*
score	*d, ∉ing, r, -board, -card, s*
scorn	*ed, ing, er, s*
scornful	*ly, ness*
scorpion	*s*
scoundrel	*s*
scour	*ed, ing, er, s*
scout	*ed, ing, er, master, s*
scowl	*ed, ing, er, s*
scragg *y*	*ier, iest, ily, iness*
scramble	*d, ∉ing, r, s*
scrap	*ped, ping, py, -book, -heap, s*
scrape	*d, ∉ing, r, s*
scratch	*ed, ing, es*
scratch *y*	*ier, iest, ily, iness*
scrawl	*ed, ing, er, s*
scrawl *y*	*ier, iest, iness*
scream	*ed, ing, er, s*
screech	*ed, ing, es*
screech *y*	*ier, iest, ily, iness*
screen	*ed, ing, s*
screw	*ed, ing, driver, s*
scribble	*d, ∉ing, r, s*

scripture	*s*
scroll	*s*
scrub	*bed, bing, ber, s*
scrum	*med, ming, mage, s*
scuffle	*d, ∉ing, r, s*
scull* (oar; to row)	*ed, ing, er, s*
sculler *y*	*ies*
sculptor	*s*
sculptress	*es*
sculpture	*d, ∉ing, s*
scuttle	*d, ∉ing, s*
scythe	*d, ∉ing, s*

se

sea*	*side, sick, shore, front, port, s*
sea*	*-gull, -horse, -lion, -serpent, s*
sea*	*man, men, -shell, -water, weed, s*
Sea Scout	*s*
seal	*ed, ing, er, skin, s*
sealing* (fastening)	*-wax*
seam* (join; rock vein)	*less, s*
search	*ed, ing, es*
searchlight	*s*
season	*-ticket, s*
seat	*ed, ing, er, -belt, s*
seclude	*d, ∉ing, s*
second	*ly, -class, -hand, -rate, s*
secondary	
secrecy	
secret	*ive, ly, s*
secretar *y*	*ies*
section	*s*
secure	*d, ∉ing, ly, ness, s*
securit *y*	*ies*
see* (notice)	*ing, s*
seed	*ed, ing, y, ling, -bed, -cake, s*

*∉ Drop **e** before adding ing*

*	scull	sea	sealing	seam
	skull	see	ceiling	seem

sh_a

seek	*ing, er, s*
seem* (appear)	*ed, ing, s*
seen* (noticed)	
see-saw	*ed, ing, s*
seize	*d, ℯing, s*
seldom	
select	*ed, ing, ion, s*
self	*-conscious, -service,* **selves**
selfish	*ly, ness*
sell* (exchange for money)	*ing, er,* * *s*
sellotape	*d, ℯing, s*
semicircle	*s*
semicircular	*ly*
semi-detached	
semolina	
send	*ing, er, s*
senior	*s*
sensation	*al, ally, s*
sense	*d, ℯing, s*
senseless	*ly, ness*
sensible	*ness*
sensibly	
sent* (send)	
sentence	*d, ℯing, s*
sentinel	*s*
sentr *y*	*ies*
separate	*d, ℯing, ly, ness, s*
separation	*s*
September	*s*
sequin	*s*
serenade	*d, ℯing, r, s*
serf* (villein; slave)	*dom, s*
sergeant	*-major, s*
serial* (in parts—as story or film)	*s*
series	
serious	*ly, ness*
sermon	*s*

serpent	*s*
servant	*-girl, s*
serve	*d, ℯing, r, s*
service	*d, ℯing, s*
serviette	*s*
session	*s*
set	*ting, ter, -square, s*
settee	*s*
settle	*d, ℯing, r, ment, s*
several	
severe	*r, st, ly*
severity	
sew* (stitch)	*ed, ing, er, s*
sewing-machine	*s*
sewn* (fastened with stitches)	
sextet(te)	*s*

sh

shabb *y*	*ier, iest, ily, iness*
shack	*s*
shade	*d, ℯing, s*
shad *y*	*ier, iest, ily, iness*
shadow	*ed, ing, s*
shadow *y*	*ily, iness*
shaft	*s*
shagg *y*	*ier, iest, ily, iness*
shake	*n, ℯing, r, s*
shak *y*	*ier, iest, ily, iness*
shall	
shallow	*er, est, ly, ness, s*
shamble	*d, ℯing, s*
shame	*d, ℯing, s*
shameful	*ly, ness*
shameless	*ly, ness*
shampoo	*ed, ing, s*
shamrock	*s*

ℯ Drop **e** before adding *ing*

*	seem	seen	sell	seller	sent	serf	serial	sew	sewn
	seam	scene	cell	cellar	scent	surf	cereal	sow, so	sown

shand y	*ies*		**shingle**	*s*
shan't (shall not)			**ship**	*ped, ping, load, mate, yard, s*
shant y	*ies*		**shipwreck**	*ed, ing, s*
shape	*d, ❬e❭ing, ly, s*		**shirk**	*ed, ing, er, s*
shapeless	*ly, ness*		**shirt**	*-button, -sleeve, -tail, s*
share	*d, ❬e❭ing, s*		**shiver**	*ed, ing, y, s*
shark	*skin, s*		**shoal**	*ed, ing, s*
sharp	*er, est, ly, ness, -shooter, s*		**shock**	*ed, ing, s*
sharpen	*ed, ing, er, s*		**shodd** y	*ier, iest, ily, iness*
shatter	*ed, ing, s*		**shoe***	*ing, -bag, horn, -lace, maker, s*
shave	*n, d, ❬e❭ing, r, s*		**shod**	
shawl	*s*		**shone**	
sheaf	**sheaves**		**shoo*** (frighten away)	*ed, ing, s*
shear* (cut; clip)	*ed, ing, er, s*		**shook**	
sheath	*s*		**shoot*** (fire)	*ing, er, s*
sheath-*knife*	*-knives*		**shop**	*ped, ping, per, keeper, lifter, s*
shed	*ding, der, s*		**shore*** (sea shore)	*s*
sheep	*-dog, -farmer, -pen, skin,* **sheep**		**shorn**	
sheer* (steep)			**short**	*age, er, est, ly, ness, bread, s*
sheet	*s*		**shorten**	*ed, ing, s*
sheik(h)	*s*		**shorthand**	
shelf	**shelves**		**shot**	*-gun, s*
shell	*ed, ing, er, s*		**should**	
shellfish	*es or* **shellfish**		**shouldn't** (should not)	
she'll (she will; she shall)			**shoulder**	*ed, ing, -bag, -blade, -strap, s*
shelter	*ed, ing, s*		**shout**	*ed, ing, er, s*
shepherd	*s*		**shovel**	*led, ling, ler, ful, s*
shepherdess	*es*		**show**	*n, ed, ing, -case, room, s*
sherbet	*s*		**show**	*-jumping, -ground, s*
sheriff	*s*		**shower**	*ed, ing, -bath, s*
sherr y	*ies*		**shower** y	*ier, iest, iness*
she's (she is; she has)			**shrank**	
shield	*ed, ing, s*		**shred**	*ded, ding, der, s*
shift	*ed, ing, y, er, s*		**shrewd**	*er, est, ly, ness*
shin	*ned, ning, -guard, -pad, s*		**shriek**	*ed, ing, er, s*
shine	*❬e❭ing, s*		**shrill**	*ed, ing, er, est, y, ness, s*
shin y	*ier, iest, ily, iness*		**shrimp**	*ed, ing, er, s or* **shrimp**

❬e❭ Drop **e** before adding *ing*

shrine	s
shrink	ing, able, age, s
shrivel	led, ling, s
shrub	s
shrubber y	ies
shrug	ged, ging, s
shrunk	en
shudder	ed, ing, s
shuffle	d, ∅ing, r, s
shun	ned, ning, s
shunt	ed, ing, er, s
shut	ting, s
shutter	ed, ing, s
shuttle	d, ∅ing, cock, s
shy	er, est, ly, ness

si

sick	er, est, ly, ness, -bay, -bed, -room
sicken	ed, ing, s
side	d, ∅ing, car, light, line, -show, s
sideboard	s
sideways	
siege	s
sieve	d, ∅ing, s
sift	ed, ing, er, s
sigh	ed, ing, s
sight* (see)	ed, ing, less, seeing, seer, s
sign	ed, ing, board, -writer, post, s
signal	led, ling, ler, man, men, s
signal-box	es
signature	-tune, s
signet* (a seal)	-ring, s
significance	
significant	ly
signify	ing
signif ied	ies

silence	d, ∅ing, r, s
silent	ly
silhouette	d, ∅ing, s
silk	en, worm, s
silk y	ier, iest, ily, iness
sill y	ier, iest, ily, iness, ies
silver	ed, ing, y, -paper, -plated
similar	ly
similarit y	ies
simmer	ed, ing, s
simple	r, st, ness, ton, -minded
simplicity	
simply	
simplify	ing
simplif ied	ication, ies
simultaneous	ly, ness
sin	ned, ning, ner, s
since	
sincere	r, st, ly, ness
sincerity	
sing	ing, er, -song, s
singe	d, ing, s
single	d, ∅ing, ∅y, -handed, s
singular	ly, s
sinister	ly
sink	ing, er, s
sip	ped, ping, per, s
siphon	ed, ing, s
sister	ly, s
sister(s)**-in-law**	
sit	ting, ter, s
sitting-room	s
site* (a place)	d, ∅ing, s
situated	
situation	s
size	d, ∅ing, s
sizzle	d, ∅ing, s

∅ Drop **e** before adding *ing*

*	sight	signet
	site	cygnet

84

sk sl

sk

skate	d, ∅ing, r, board, s
skating-rink	s
skein	s
skeleton	s
sketch	ed, ing, es
sketch y	ier, iest, ily, iness
skewer	ed, ing, s
ski	-ed, -ing, er, -jump, -lift, -run, s
skid	ded, ding, s
skilful	ly, ness
skill	ed, s
skim	med, ming, mer, s
skin	ned, ning, -diving, -diver, s
skinn y	ier, iest, iness
skip	ped, ping, per, s
skipping-rope	s
skipper	ed, ing, s
skirmish	ed, ing, es
skirt	ed, ing, s
skittle	d, ∅ing, r, -alley, -ball, -pin, s
skull* (head bones)	-cap, s
skulk	ed, ing, s
skunk	s
sky	ing, lark, light, -rocket, scraper
sk ied	ies

sl

slack	ed, ing, er, est, ly, ness, s
slacken	ed, ing, s
slain	
slam	med, ming, s
slang	ing, y
slant	ed, ing, wise, s
slap	ped, ping, per, dash, stick, s
slash	ed, ing, es

slate	s
slaughter	ed, ing, er, -house, s
slave	d, ∅ing, r, ry, -driver, -trader, s
slay* (kill)	ing, er, s
sledge	d, ∅ing, r, s
sleek	ed, ing, er, est, ly, ness, s
sleep	ing, er, less, -walking, -walker, s
sleep y	ier, iest, ily, iness
slept	
sleet	ed, ing, s
sleet y	ier, iest, iness
sleeve	d, less, -button, s
sleigh* (sledge)	ing, -bell, -horse, s
slender	ly, ness
sleuth	-hound, s
slew	
slice	d, ∅ing, r, s
slick	ed, ing, er, est, ly, ness, s
slid	
slide	∅ing, r, s
slight	ed, ing, er, est, ly, ness, s
slim	med, ming, mer, mest, ly, ness, s
slime	
slim y	ier, iest, ily, iness
sling	ing, er, s
slink	ing, er, s
slink y	ier, iest, ily, iness
slip	ped, ping, knot, shod, way, s
slipper	s
slipper y	ier, iest, ily, iness
slit	ting, ter, s
slither	ed, ing, y, s
sloe* (wild plum)	-tree, s
slog	ged, ging, ger, s
slogan	s
slop	ped, ping, -basin, s
slopp y	ier, iest, ily, iness

∅ Drop e before adding ing

*	skull		slay	sloe
	scull		sleigh	slow

sm

slope	d, ǿing, s
slot	ted, ting, -machine, -meter, s
slouch	ed, ing, es
slovenly	ier, iest, iness
slow*	ed, ing, er, est, ly, ness, s
slow-worm	s
slug	s
sluggish	ly, ness
sluice	d, ǿing, -gate, s
slum	my, -dweller, s
slumber	ed, ing, er, s
slump	ed, ing, s
slung	
slunk	
slush	ed, ing, es
slushy	ier, iest, ily, iness
sly	er, est, ly, ness

sm

smack	ed, ing, s
small	er, est, ness
smart	ed, ing, er, est, ly, ness, s
smarten	ed, ing, s
smash	ed, ing, es
smear	ed, ing, s
smeary	ier, iest, ily, iness
smell	ed, ing, er, s
smelly	ier, iest, ily, iness
smelt or **smelled**	
smile	d, ǿing, r, s
smirk	ed, ing, er, s
smithereens	
smock	ed, ing, s
smoke	d, ǿing, r, -bomb, -screen, s
smoky	ier, iest, ily, iness
smooth	ed, ing, er, est, ly, ness, s

sn

smother	ed, ing, s
smoulder	ed, ing, s
smudge	d, ǿing, s
smudgy	ier, iest, ily, iness
smuggle	d, ǿing, r, s
smut	ted, ting, s
smutty	ier, iest, ily, iness

sn

snack	-bar, s
snail	s
snake	d, ǿing, ǿy, -bite, -charmer, s
snap	ped, ping, per, shot, dragon, s
snare	d, ǿing, r, s
snarl	ed, ing, er, s
snatch	ed, ing, es
sneak	ed, ing, er, s
sneaky	ier, iest, ily, iness
sneer	ed, ing, er, s
sneeze	d, ǿing, r, s
sniff	ed, ing, er, s
sniffle	d, ǿing, r, s
snigger	ed, ing, er, s
snip	ped, ping, per, s
snipe	d, ǿing, r, s
snivel	led, ling, ler, s
snob	bery, bish, bishness, s
snooker	ed
snore	d, ǿing, r, s
snort	ed, ing, er, s
snow	ed, ing, drift, fall, flake, storm, s
snow	man, men, -plough, drop, shoe, s
snowball	ed, ing, s
snowy	ier, iest, ily, iness
snug	ger, gest, ly, ness
snuggle	d, ǿing, s

ǿ Drop **e** before adding *ing*

* slow
  sloe

so

sp_a

soak	ed, ing, s
soap	ed, ing, -suds, -bubble, -flake, s
soapy	ier, iest, ily, iness
soar* (fly upwards)	ed, ing, s
sob	bed, bing, s
sociable	ness
social	ly, s
socialist	s
society	ies
sock	s
socket	s
soda	-bread, -fountain, -water
sodden	
sofa	s
soft	er, est, ish, ly, ness, -hearted
soften	ed, ing, er, s
soggy	ier, iest, ily, iness
soil	ed, ing, s
sold* (sell)	
solder	ed, ing, s
soldier	ed, ing, s
sole* (only)	ly
sole* (bottom-of shoe, etc.)	d,* ǿing, s
sole* (fish)	s or **sole**
solemn	ity, ly, ness
solicitor	s
solid	ity, ly, s
solitary	
solo	ist, -singer, s
solution	s
solve	d, ǿing, s
some*	body, one, how, thing, where
sometime	s
somersault	ed, ing, s
son* (boy)	ny, s
song	ster, -book, -bird, -writer, s

soon	er, est
soot	
sooty	ier, iest, ily, iness
soothe	d, ǿing, s
soprano	s
sore* (painful)	r, st, ly, ness, s
sorrow	ed, ing, ful, fully, s
sorry	ier, iest, ily, iness
sort	ed, ing, er, s
soul* (spirit)	ful, fully, s
sound	ed, ing, er, est, ly, ness, s
soup	-plate, -spoon, s
sour	ed, ing, er, est, ly, ness, s
source	s
south	-east, -west, ern, erly, ward
souvenir	s
sovereign	s
sow* (scatter seed)	ed, ing, er, s
sown* (planted)	

sp

space	d, ǿing, r, s, craft, man, men
space	-capsule, ship, -station, suit, s
spacious	ly, ness
spade	ful, s
spaghetti	
span	ned, ning, s
spangle	d, ǿing, s
spaniel	s
spank	ed, ing, s
spanner	s
spare	d, ǿing, s
spark	ed, ing, s
sparkle	d, ǿing, r, s
sparrow	-hawk, s
spastic	s

ǿ Drop **e** before adding *ing*

*	soar	sold	sole	some	son	sow	sown
	sore	soled	soul	sum	sun	sew	sewn
						so	

spe   sph   spi   spl   spo   spr   spu   spy

spat		**splash**		*ed, ing, es*
spawn	*ed, ing, s*	**splendid**		*ly*
speak	*ing, er, s*	**splendour**		*s*
spear	*ed, ing, man, men, head, -gun, s*	**splint**		*s*
special	*ly, ty, ist, ity*	**splinter**		*ed, ing, y, s*
specialize	*d, ǿing, s*	**split**		*ting, ter, s*
specimen	*s*	**splutter**		*ed, ing, er, s*
speck	*ed, ing, less, lessly, s*	**spoil**		*ed, ing, er, -sport, s*
speckle	*d, ǿing, s*	**spoilt** or **spoiled**		
spectacle	*s*	**spoke** (speak)		*n, sman, smen*
spectacular	*ly*	**spoke** (of wheel)		*s*
spectator	*s*	**sponge**		*d, ǿing, r, -bag, -cake, s*
spectre	*s*	**spong** *y*		*ier, iest, ily, iness*
sped or **speeded**		**spool**		*s*
speech	*-training, less, es*	**spoon**		*ed, ing, ful, s*
speed	*ed, ing, -boat, -limit, way, s*	**sport**		*ed, ing, sman, smen, s*
speed *y*	*ier, iest, ily, iness*	**sport** *y*		*ier, iest, ily, iness*
spell	*ed, ing, er, bind, bound, s*	**spot**		*ted, ting, ter, less, lessly, light, s*
spelt or **spelled**		**spott** *y*		*ier, iest, ily, iness*
spend	*ing, er, thrift, s*	**spout**		*ed, ing, s*
spent		**sprain**		*ed, ing, s*
sphere	*s*	**sprang**		
spider	*y, s*	**sprat**		*s* or **sprat**
spied		**sprawl**		*ed, ing, er, s*
spike	*d, ǿing, s*	**spray**		*ed, ing, er, s*
spill	*ed, ing, s*	**spread**		*ing, er, s*
spilt or **spilled**		**spring**		*ing, -cleaning, -board, time, s*
spin	*ning, ner, -dryer, s*	**spring** *y*		*ier, iest, ily, iness*
spinach		**sprinkle**		*d, ǿing, r, s*
spinster	*s*	**sprint**		*ed, ing, er, s*
spiral	*led, ling, ly, s*	**sprout**		*ed, ing, s*
spire	*s*	**sprung**		
spirit	*ed, ing, -level, -lamp, s*	**spun**		
spirt or **spurt**	*ed, ing, s*	**spur**		*red, ring, s*
spit	*ting, ter, s*	**spurt** or **spirt**		*ed, ing, s*
spite	*d, ǿing, s*	**spy**		*ing*
spiteful	*ly, ness*	**sp** *ied*		*ies*

ǿ Drop **e** before adding *ing*

sq st_a

ste

sq

squabble	d, ǿing, r, s
squad	ron, s
squall	ed, ing, y, s
squander	ed, ing, er, s
square	d, ǿing, ly, ness, -dance, root, s
squash	ed, ing, y, es
squat	ted, ting, ter, s
squaw	s
squawk	ed, ing, er, s
squeak	ed, ing, er, s
squeak y	ier, iest, ily, iness
squeal	ed, ing, er, s
squeeze	d, ǿing, r, s
squelch	ed, ing, es
squib	s
squint	ed, ing, er, s
squire	d, ǿing, s
squirm	ed, ing, er, s
squirrel	s
squirt	ed, ing, er, s

st

stab	bed, bing, ber, s
stable	d, ǿing, -man, -men, -boy, s
stack	ed, ing, s
stadium	s or **stadia**
staff	ed, ing, -room, s
stag	-beetle, -horn, hound, -hunt, s
stage	d, ǿing, -hand, -manager, s
stage-coach	es
stagger	ed, ing, er, s
stain	ed, ing, less, er, s
stair*	-carpet, case, -rod, way, s
stake* (a stick; bet)	d, ǿing, s
stale	r, st, ly, ness

stalk	ed, ing, er, s
stall	ed, ing, -holder, s
stallion	s
stammer	ed, ing, er, s
stamp	ed, ing, -album, -collector, s
stampede	d, ǿing, s
stand	ing, s
standard	-bearer, s
star	red, ring, less, light, lit, s
starr y	ier, iest, ily, iness
starboard	
starfish	es or **starfish**
starch	ed, ing, es
stare* (look at)	d, ǿing, s
starling	s
start	ed, ing, er, s
startle	d, ǿing, s
starvation	
starve	d, ǿing, s
state	d, ǿing, ment, s
statel y	ier, iest, ily, iness
station	ed, ing, -master, s
stationary* (still)	
stationer	s
stationery* (paper, pens, etc.)	
statue	tte, s
staunch	ed, ing, er, est, ly, ness, es
stay	ed, ing, er, s
steady	ing
stead ied	ier, iest, ily, iness, ies
steak* (meat)	s
steal* (thieve)	ing, s
stealth	
stealth y	ier, iest, ily, iness
steam	ed, ing, er, boat, ship, -engine, s
steam y	ier, iest, ily, iness
steel* (metal)	ed, ing, y, work, worker, s

ǿ Drop **e** before adding *ing*

stationary	steal
stationery	steel

sti   sto   str

steep	er, est, ly, ness	**stool**	-ball, s
steeple	chase, jack, s	**stoop**	ed, ing, s
steer	age, ed, ing, er, sman, smen, s	**stop**	ped, ping, page, per, s
steering-wheel	s	**storage**	
stem	med, ming, s	**store**	d, ⌀ing, house, keeper, -room, s
stencil	led, ling, ler, s	**storey*** (floor)	s
step	ped, ping, -ladder, s	**stork**	s
step	father, mother, brother, sister, s	**storm**	ed, ing, -cloud, s
stepping-stone	s	**storm** y	ier, iest, ily, iness
sterilize	d, ⌀ing, r, s	**stor** y* (tale; floor)	ies
stern	er, est, ly, ness	**stout**	er, est, ly, ness, ish, hearted
stew	ed, ing, er, -pot, s	**stove**	-pipe, s
steward	s	**stow**	ed, ing, away, s
stewardess	es	**straggle**	d, ⌀ing, r, s
stick	ing, er, -insect, s	**straight*** (not bent)	er, est, ly, ness
stick y	ier, iest, ily, iness	**straighten**	ed, ing, er, s
stickleback	s	**strain**	ed, ing, er, s
stiff	er, est, ly, ness	**strait*** (sea channel)	s
stiffen	ed, ing, er, s	**strand**	ed, ing, s
stifle	d, ⌀ing, r, s	**strange**	r, st, ly, ness
stile* (steps)	s	**stranger**	s
still	ed, ing, ness, s	**strangle**	d, ⌀ing, hold, r, s
sting	ing, er, s	**strap**	ped, ping, less, s
stinging-nettle	s	**straw**	board, -coloured, -hat, s
stir	red, ring, rer, s	**strawberr** y	ies
stirrup	s	**stray**	ed, ing, er, s
stitch	ed, ing, es	**streak**	ed, ing, er, s
stoat	s	**streak** y	ier, iest, ily, iness
stock	ed, ing, ist, -car, -pot, -room, s	**stream**	ed, ing, lined, er, s
stocking	s	**street**	-sweeper, s
stockade	d, ⌀ing, s	**strength**	s
stoke	d, ⌀ing, r, s	**strengthen**	ed, ing, er, s
stole	n	**strenuous**	ly, ness
stomach	-ache, -pump, s	**stretch**	ed, ing, es
stone	d, ⌀ing, -cold, -deaf, -mason, s	**stretcher**	-bearer, s
ston y	ier, iest, ily, iness	**strict**	er, est, ly, ness
stood		**stride**	⌀ing, r, s

⌀ Drop **e** before adding *ing*

strike	*∉ing, r, s*
string	*ing, -bag, -vest, s*
strip	*ped, ping, per, -lighting, s*
stripe	*d, ∉ing, s*
strode	
stroke	*d, ∉ing, r, s*
stroll	*ed, ing, er, s*
strong	*er, est, ly, ish, hold, -room*
struck	
structure	*s*
struggle	*d, ∉ing, r, s*
strum	*med, ming, mer, s*
strung	
strut	*ted, ting, ter, s*
stub	*bed, bing, by, s*
stubborn	*ly, ness*
stuck	
stud	*ded, ding, s*
student	*s*
studio	*s*
studious	*ly, ness*
study	*ing*
stud *ied*	*ies*
stuff	*ed, ing, er, s*
stuff *y*	*ier, iest, ily, iness*
stumble	*d, ∉ing, r, s*
stump	*ed, ing, s*
stump *y*	*ier, iest, ily, iness*
stun	*ned, ning, ner, s*
stung	
stunt	*ed, ing, man, men, s*
stupendous	*ly, ness*
stupid	*ity, ly*
sturd *y*	*ier, iest, ily, iness*
stutter	*ed, ing, er, s*
st *y*	*ies*
style* (way; fashion)	*d, ∉ing, s*

su

subject	*ed, ing, s*
submarine	*r, s*
submerge	*d, ∉ing, s*
submit	*ted, ting, s*
subscribe	*d, ∉ing, r, s*
subscription	*s*
subside	*d, ∉ing, s*
substance	*s*
substantial	*ly*
substitute	*d, ∉ing, s*
subtract	*ed, ing, ion, s*
suburb	*s*
succeed	*ed, ing, s*
success	*es*
successful	*ly*
succession	*s*
successor	*s*
such	*like*
suck	*ed, ing, er, s*
suction	*-pump*
sudden	*ly, ness*
suds	
suet	*-pudding, y*
suffer	*ed, ing, er, s*
sufficient	*ly*
suffocate	*d, ∉ing, s*
suffocation	
sugar	*ed, ing, y, -basin, -beet, -cane, s*
suggest	*ed, ing, ion, s*
suicide	*s*
suit	*ed, ing, able, ably, ability, case, s*
suite* (set of furniture, rooms, etc.)	*s*
sulk	*ed, ing, s*
sulk *y*	*ier, iest, ily, iness*
sullen	*ly, ness*
sultana	*s*

∉ Drop **e** before adding *ing*

*****	style	suite
	stile	sweet

SW

sum* (add up; total)	*med, ming, s*
summer	*y, -time, -house, s*
summit	*s*
summon	*ed, ing, s*
summons	*es*
sumptuous	*ly, ness*
sun*	*ned, ning, beam, light, flower, s*
sun*	*-glasses, rise, set, shine, shade, s*
sunny	*ier, iest, ily, iness*
sunbathe	*d, ∅ing, r, s*
sunburn	*ed, t*
sundae* (ice cream)	*s*
Sunday*	*-school, s*
sung	
sunk	*en*
superb	*ly*
superintend	*ed, ing, ent, s*
superior	*ity, s*
supermarket	*s*
superstition	*s*
superstitious	*ly, ness*
supervise	*d, ∅ing, s*
supervision	
supervisor	*s*
supper	*-time, s*
supple	*ness*
supply	*ing*
supplied	*ier, ies*
support	*ed, ing, er, s*
suppose	*d, ∅ing, s*
sure* (certain)	*r, st, ly, ness, -footed*
surf* (sea foam)	*ing, -board, -riding*
surface	*d, ∅ing, s*
surge	*d, ∅ing, s*
surgeon	*s*
surgery	*ies*
surname	*s*

surplice* (gown)	*s*
surplus* (left over)	*es*
surprise	*d, ∅ing, s*
surrender	*ed, ing, s*
surround	*ed, ing, s*
survey	*ed, ing, or, s*
survival	
survive	*d, ∅ing, s*
survivor	*s*
suspect	*ed, ing, s*
suspend	*ed, ing, er, s*
suspense	
suspicion	*s*
suspicious	*ly, ness*
sustain	*ed, ing, s*

SW

swagger	*ed, ing, er, -cane, -coat, -stick, s*
swallow	*ed, ing, er, s*
swam	
swamp	*ed, ing, s*
swampy	*ier, iest, ily, iness*
swan	*s*
swap or **swop**	*ped, ping, per, s*
swarm	*ed, ing, s*
swarthy	*ier, iest, ily, iness*
sway	*ed, ing, s*
swear	*ing, er, -word, s*
sweat	*ed, ing, y, er, -band, -shirt, -suit, s*
swede	*s*
sweep	*ing, er, stake, s*
swept	
sweet*	*er, est, ish, ly, ness, heart, -pea, s*
sweeten	*ed, ing, er, s*
swell	*ed, ing, s*
swelter	*ed, ing, s*

*∅ Drop **e** before adding *ing**

* sum	sun	sundae	sure	surf	surplice	sweet
some	son	Sunday	shore	serf	surplus	suite

sy   ta

		ta	
swept		**tabby-cat**	*s*
swerve	*d, ∅ing, s*	**table**	*-tennis, -cloth, -mat, s*
swift	*er, est, ly, ness, s*	**table-spoon**	*ful, s*
swill	*ed, ing, s*	**tableau**	*x or s*
swim	*mer, suit, s*	**tablet**	*s*
swimming	*-bath, -pool*	**tack**	*ed, ing, s*
swindle	*d, ∅ing, r, s*	**tackle**	*d, ∅ing, r, s*
swine	*herd.* **swine**	**tact**	*ful, fully, less, lessly*
swing	*ing, er, s*	**tactics**	
swipe	*d, ∅ing, r, s*	**tadpole**	*s*
swirl	*ed, ing, s*	**tag**	*ged, ging, s*
swish	*ed, ing, es*	**tail***	*ed, ing, -end, -lamp, -light, -spin, s*
switch	*ed, ing, es*	**tailor**	*ed, ing, -made, s*
swivel	*led, ling, s*	**take**	*n, ∅ing, r, -away, -off, s*
swollen		**talcum powder**	
swoon	*ed, ing, s*	**tale*** (story)	*-bearer, -teller, s*
swoop	*ed, ing, s*	**talent**	*ed, s*
swop or **swap**	*ped, ping, per, s*	**talk**	*ative, ed, ing, er, s*
sword	*sman, smen, -dance, s*	**tall**	*er, est, ish, ness*
swordfish	*es* or **swordfish**	**tambourine**	*s*
swore		**tame**	*d, ∅ing, r, st, ly, ness, s*
sworn		**tamper**	*ed, ing, er, s*
swum		**tan**	*ned, ning, ner, s*
swung		**tandem**	*s*
		tangerine	*s*
	sy	**tangle**	*d, ∅ing, s*
sycamore	*-tree, s*	**tango**	*ed, ing, s*
sympathetic	*ally*	**tank**	*er, ful, -trap, s*
sympathize	*d, ∅ing, r, s*	**tankard**	*s*
sympath *y*	*ies*	**tantalize**	*d, ∅ing, s*
symphon *y*	*ies*	**tantrum**	*s*
symptom	*s*	**tap**	*ped, ping, per, -dance, -dancing, s*
synagogue	*s*	**tape**	*d, ∅ing, s*
syringe	*d, ∅ing, s*	**tape**	*-measure, -recorder, -recording, s*
syrup	*y*	**tapestr** *y*	*ies*
system	*atic, atically, s*	**tapioca**	

∅ Drop **e** *before adding ing*

* tail
* tale

te

tar	red, ring, ry, s
tarantula	s
tare* (weed)	s
target	s
tarnish	ed, ing, es
tarpaulin	s
tart	let, s
tartan	s
task	ed, ing, master, s
tassel	s
taste	d, ℓing, r, s
tasteful	ly, ness
tasteless	ly, ness
tatter	ed, ing, s
tattoo	ed, ing, er, ist, -mark, s
taught* (teach)	
taunt	ed, ing, er, s
taut* (tight)	er, est, ly, ness
tavern	s
tax	ation, ed, ing, es
taxi	-cab, -driver, -rank, s

te

tea*	cake, -cloth, cup, pot, -service, s
tea*	-set, -things, -time, -table, -tray, s
tea-cosy	ies
tea-leaf	-leaves
tea-party	ies
tea-spoon	ful, s
teach	ing, ings, es
teacher	s
teak	
team* (side; number)	-work, s
tear* (pull apart)	ing, s
tear	-gas, -drop, s
tearful	ly, ness

tease	d, ℓing, r, s
technical	ly
technician	s
Teddy bear	s
tedious	ly, ness
tee* (golf)	d, ing, -shot, s
tee-shirt or **T-shirt**	s
teem* (pour; swarm)	ed, ing, s
teenage	d, -boy, -girl
teenager	s
teeth	
telegram	s
telegraph	ed, ing, -line, -pole, -wire, s
telephone	d, ℓing, s
telescope	d, ℓing, s
televise	d, ℓing, s
television	s
tell	ing, er, -tale, s
temper	ed, ing, s
temperature	s
temple	s
temporary	ily
tempt	ation, ed, ing, er, s
tend	ed, ing, s
tender	-hearted, ly, ness
tenement	s
tennis	-ball, -court, -racket
tenor	s
tense	d, ℓing, r, st, ly, ness, s
tent	-peg, -pole, -rope, s
tentacle	s
tepid	ly, ness
term	ly, ed, ing, s
terminus	es or **termini**
terrace	d, ℓing, -house, s
terrible	ness
terribly	

ℓ Drop **e** before adding ing

* tare	taught	tea	team
tear	taut	tee	teem

th

terrier	*s*
terrific	*ally*
terrify	*ing*
terrif *ied*	*ies*
territorial	*s*
territor *y*	*ies*
terror	*ism, ist, -stricken, s*
terrorize	*d, ∮ing, s*
test	*ed, ing, -paper, -piece, -tube, s*
testament	*s*
testimonial	*s*
tetanus	
tether	*ed, ing, s*
text	*-book, s*
textile	*s*

th

than	
thank	*ed, ing, -offering, s*
thankful	*ly, ness*
thankless	*ly, ness*
that	
that's (that is)	
thatch	*ed, ing, es*
thaw	*ed, ing, s*
theatre	*-ticket, s*
theatrical	*ly, s*
theft	*s*
their* (belonging to them)	
theirs* (belonging to them)	
them	*selves*
then	
theor *y*	*ies*
there* (in that place)	*abouts, after*
therefore	
there's* (there is)	

thermometer	*s*
thermos flask	*s*
these	
they	
they'll (they will; they shall)	
they're* (they are)	
they've (they have)	
thick	*er, est, ly, ness, ish, -skinned*
thicken	*ed, ing, er, s*
thicket	*s*
thief	**thieves**
thieve	*d, ∮ing, s*
thimble	*ful, s*
thin	*ned, ning, ner, nest, ly, ness, s*
thing	*s*
think	*ing, er, s*
thirst	*ed, ing, s*
thirst *y*	*ier, iest, ily, iness*
this	
thistle	*s*
thorn	*s*
thorn *y*	*ier, iest, ily, iness*
thorough	*ly, ness, bred, fare*
those	
though	
thought	*-reader, s*
thoughtful	*ly, ness*
thoughtless	*ly, ness*
thrash	*ed, ing, ings, es*
thread	*ed, ing, bare, er, s*
threat	*s*
threaten	*ed, ing, s*
thresh	*ed, ing, es*
threw* (throw)	
thrift	*less*
thrift *y*	*ier, iest, ily, iness*
thrill	*ed, ing, er, s*

∮ Drop **e** *before adding* ing

*	their	theirs		threw
	there	there's		through
	they're			

ti   to

thrive	*d, øing, s*
throat	*s*
throb	*bed, bing, s*
throne* (king's seat)	*s*
throng	*ed, ing, s*
throttle	*d, øing, s*
through* (from end to end)	*out*
throw	*ing, er, n,* s*
thrush	*es*
thrust	*ing, s*
thud	*ded, ding, s*
thug	*s*
thumb	*ed, ing, -mark, -nail, screw, s*
thump	*ed, ing, er, s*
thunder	*ed, ing, y, bolt, clap, storm, s*
Thursday	*s*

ti

tiara	*s*
tick	*ed, ing, s*
ticket	*-collector, -office, s*
tickle	*d, øing, r, s*
ticklish	*ly, ness*
tide* (sea)	*-mark, s*
tidings	
tidy	*ing*
tid *ied*	*ier, iest, ily, iness, ies*
tie	*d,* -clip, -pin, s*
tying	
tiger	*-cat, -moth, s*
tigress	*es*
tight *er, est, ly, ness, -rope, s*	
tighten	*ed, ing, er, s*
tile	*d, øing, r, s*
till	*ed, ing, er, s*
till or **until**	

tilt	*ed, ing, er, s*
timber	*ed, -mill, -yard, s*
time	*d, øing, r, ly, less, -bomb, table, s*
timid	*ity, ly, ness*
tin	*ned, ning, ny, -opener, foil, -tack, s*
tinge	*d, øing, s*
tingle	*d, øing, s*
tinker	*ed, ing, s*
tinkle	*d, øing, s*
tinsel	*led, ling, ly*
tint	*ed, ing, s*
tin *y*	*ier, iest, ily, iness*
tip	*ped, ping, per, ster, s*
tiptoe	*d, ing, s*
tire* (weary)	*d, øing, some, s*
tired	*ness*
tireless	*ly, ness*
tissue	*-paper, s*
title	*d, s*
titter	*ed, ing, s*

to

to* (towards)	
toad	*-in-the-hole, s*
toadstool	*s*
to and fro	
toast	*ed, ing, er, -rack, s*
tobacco	*nist, -pipe, -plant, s*
toboggan	*ed, ing, er, s*
today or **to-day**	
toddle	*d, øing, r, s*
toe*	*d, ing, -cap, -hold, -nail, s*
toffee	*-apple, s*
together	*ness*
toil	*ed, ing, er, s*
toilet	*-paper, -roll, -soap, s*

*ø Drop **e** before adding* ing

*	throne	through	tide	tire	toe	to
	thrown	threw	tied	tyre	tow	too
						two (2)

token	s	**toss**	ed, ing, es	
told		**total**	led, ling, ly, s	
tolerate	d, ∅ing, s	**totter**	ed, ing, y, er, s	
toll	ed, ing, -bridge, -gate, s	**touch**	ed, ing, y, es	
tomahawk	s	**tough**	er, est, ly, ness, s	
tomato	es	**toughen**	ed, ing, s	
tomb	stone, s	**tour**	ed, ing, ist, s	
tomcat	s	**tournament**	s	
tomorrow or **to-morrow**	s	**tousle**	d, ∅ing, s	
tomtit	s	**tow*** (pull)	ed, ing, -line, -path, -rope, s	
ton or **tonne** (metric)	s	**towards** or **toward**		
tone	d, ∅ing, -deaf, s	**towel**	led, ling, -rail, s	
tongs		**tower**	ed, ing, -block, s	
tongue	-tied, -twister, s	**town**	-council, -crier, -hall, s	
tonic	s	**toy**	ed, ing, shop, s	
tonight or **to-night**				
tonsil	s			
tonsillitis		**tr**		
too* (more than enough; also)		**trace**	d, ∅ing, r, s	
took		**tracing-paper**		
tool	-bag, -chest, -shed, s	**track**	ed, ing, er, suit, s	
tooth	ache, paste, powder, less, **teeth**	**tractor**	s	
tooth-brush	es	**trade**	d, ∅ing, mark, sman, smen, r, s	
top	ped, ping, per, knot, -heavy, -hat, s	**traffic**	-sign, -signal, -lights	
topic	s	**traged**y	ies	
topple	d, ∅ing, s	**tragic**	ally	
topsy-turvy		**trail**	ed, ing, er, s	
torch	es	**train**	ed, ing, er, s	
tore		**traitor**	ous, ously, s	
torment	ed, ing, or, s	**tramp**	ed, ing, er, s	
torn		**trample**	d, ∅ing, r, s	
tornado	es	**trampoline**	s	
torpedo	ed, ing, es	**transfer**	red, ring, able, s	
torrent	s	**transform**	ed, ing, ation, s	
torrential	ly	**transistor**	-radio, s	
tortoise	-shell, s	**translate**	d, ∅ing, s	
torture	d, ∅ing, r, -chamber, s	**translation**	s	

∅ Drop **e** before adding *ing*

*   too   tow
     to   toe
     two (2)

tre   tri   tro   tru   try

transparent	*ly, ness*
transport	*ed, ing, er, ation, able, s*
trap	*ped, ping, per, -door, s*
trapeze	*s*
travel	*led, ling, ler, s*
trawl	*ed, ing, er, s*
tray	*-cloth, ful, s*
treacherous	*ly, ness*
treacher *y*	*ies*
treacle	
tread	*ing, s*
treason	*able*
treasure	*d, ø̸ing, r, -chest, -hunt, s*
treat	*ed, ing, ment, s*
treble	*d, ø̸ing, s*
tree	*-stump, -top, -trunk, s*
trek	*ked, king, ker, s*
trellis	*-work*
tremble	*d, ø̸ing, s*
tremendous	*ly, ness*
trench	*es*
trespass	*ed, ing, es*
trespasser	*s*
trestle	*-table, s*
trial	*s*
triangle	*s*
tribe	*sman, smen, s*
tributar *y*	*ies*
trick	*ed, ing, ery, ster, s*
trick *y*	*ier, iest, ily, iness*
trickle	*d, ø̸ing, s*
tricycle	*d, ø̸ing, s*
tried	
trier	*s*
tries	
trifle	*d, ø̸ing, s*
trigger	*ed, ing, s*

trim	*med, ming, mer, mest, ly, ness, s*
trinket	*s*
trio	*s*
trip	*ped, ping, per, s*
triple	*d, ø̸ing, s*
triplet	*s*
tripod	*s*
triumph	*ed, ing, ant, antly, s*
trod	*den*
trolley	*s*
trombone	*ø̸ist, s*
troop* (of scouts, soldiers)	*ed, ing, er, s*
troph *y*	*ies*
tropic	*al, ally, s*
trot	*ted, ting, ter, s*
trouble	*d, ø̸ing, some, -maker, s*
trough	*s*
troupe* (of entertainers)	*r, s*
trousers	
trousseau	*x or s*
trout	**trout**
trowel	*s*
truant	*s*
truck	*-load, s*
trudge	*d, ø̸ing, s*
true	*r, st, ness*
truly	
trumpet	*ed, ing, er, -call, s*
truncheon	*s*
trunk	*s*
truss	*ed, ing, es*
trust	*ed, ing, worthy, s*
trust *y*	*ier, iest, ily, iness*
truth	*s*
truthful	*ly, ness*
try	*ing*
tr *ied*	*ier, ies*

ø̸ Drop **e** before adding *ing*

*   troop
     troupe

tu tw ty ug um

tu

tuba	s
tubb y	ier, iest, iness
tube	øing, less, -train, s
tuck	ed, ing, -shop, s
Tudor	s
Tuesday	s
tuft	s
tug	ged, ging, ger, boat, s
tug-of-war	
tuition	
tulip	s
tumble	d, øing, r, down, -dryer, s
tumbler	ful, s
tumult	s
tumultuous	ly, ness
tundra	s
tune	d, øing, r, s
tuneful	ly, ness
tuneless	ly, ness
tunic	s
tunnel	led, ling, ler, s
turban	s
turbine	s
turf	ed, ing, s or **turves**
turkey	cock, s
Turkish delight	
turmoil	
turn	ed, ing, er, over, stile, table, s
turnip	s
turpentine	
turquoise	s
turret	ed, s
turtle	-neck, -shell, -soup, -dove, s
tusk	s
tussle	d, øing, s
tutor	ial, s

tw

twang	ed, ing, s
tweed	s
tweezers	
twice	
twiddle	d, øing, r, s
twig	s
twilight	
twin	ned, ning, -brother, -sister, s
twine	d, øing, s
twinge	d, øing, s
twinkle	d, øing, s
twirl	ed, ing, s
twist	ed, ing, er, s
twist y	ier, iest, ily, iness
twitch	ed, ing, es
twitter	ed, ing, s

ty

tying	
type	d, øing, written, writing, writer, s
typist	s
typhoon	s
typical	ly, ness
tyrannize	d, øing, s
tyrant	s
tyre* (wheel cover)	s

ug

ugl y	ier, iest, ily, iness

um

umbrella	-stand, s
umpire	d, øing, s

ø Drop e before adding ing

*   tyre
     tire

un

un	
unable	
unafraid	
unaided	
unarm	*ed, ing, s*
unattractive	*ly, ness*
unavoidable	*y*
unaware	*s*
unbalance	*d, ∮ing, s*
unbearable	*y*
unbeaten	
unbolt	*ed, ing, s*
unbuckle	*d, ∮ing, s*
unbutton	*ed, ing, s*
uncanny	*ily, iness*
uncertain	*ly, ty*
uncivilized	
uncle	*s*
unclean	*liness*
uncomfortable	*ness*
uncommon	*ly, ness*
unconscious	*ly, ness*
uncork	*ed, ing, s*
uncover	*ed, ing, s*
uncurl	*ed, ing, s*
undamaged	
undecided	*ly*
under	*clothes, clothing, wear*
under	*go, going, goes, gone, went*
undercurrent	*s*
underground	
undergrowth	
underneath	
understand	*able, ing, s*
understood	
understudy	*ing*
understudied	*ies*

undertake	*n, ∮ing, r, s*
undertook	
undid	
undo	*ing*
undone	
undoubted	*ly*
undress	*ed, ing, es*
uneasy	*ier, iest, ily, iness*
unemployed	*ment*
uneven	*ly, ness*
unexpected	*ly, ness*
unexplored	
unfair	*ly, ness*
unfasten	*ed, ing, s*
unfinished	
unfit	*ted, ting, s*
unfold	*ed, ing, s*
unfortunate	*ly*
unfriendly	*iness*
unfurnished	
ungrateful	*ly, ness*
unguarded	*ly, ness*
unhappy	*ier, iest, ily, iness*
unharmed	
unhealthy	*ier, iest, ily, iness*
unhurt	
uniform	*ed, s*
unimportant	
uninhabited	
uninjured	
uninteresting	
Union Jack	*s*
unite	*d, ∮ing, s*
universe	
university	*ies*
unjust	*ly, ness*
unkind	*er, est, ly, ness*

∮ Drop **e** before adding *ing*

up   ur   us

unknown	
unlawful	*ly, ness*
unless	
unlike	*ness*
unlikel *y*	*ier, iest, ihood*
unload	*ed, ing, s*
unlock	*ed, ing, s*
unluck *y*	*ier, iest, ily, iness*
unmistakabl *e*	*y*
unnecessar *y*	*ily*
unoccupied	
unpack	*ed, ing, s*
unpleasant	*ly, ness*
unpopular	*ity, ly*
unravel	*led, ling, s*
unreasonabl *e*	*y*
unreliable	*ness*
unroll	*ed, ing, s*
unsaddle	*d, ∅ing, s*
unsafe	*r, st, ly, ness*
unscrew	*ed, ing, s*
unselfish	*ly, ness*
unstead *y*	*ier, iest, ily, iness*
unsuitable	
untangle	*d, ∅ing, s*
untid *y*	*ier, iest, ily, iness*
untie	*d, s*
untying	
until or till	
untrue	
unusual	*ly, ness*
unveil	*ed, ing, s*
unwelcome	
unwell	
unwilling	*ly, ness*
unwise	*ly*
unwrap	*ped, ping, s*

up

upbringing	
upheaval	*s*
upholster	*ed, ing, er, s*
upholster *y*	*ies*
upkeep	
upon	
upper	*most, -cut, s*
upright	*ly, ness, s*
uprising	*s*
uproar	*s*
uproot	*ed, ing, s*
upset	*ting, s*
upside-down	
upstairs	
upstream	
upturn	*ed, ing, s*
upward	*ly, s*

ur

uranium	
urban	
urchin	*s*
urge	*d, ∅ing, s*
urgenc *y*	*ies*
urgent	*ly*
urn* (vase; tea-urn)	*s*

us

use	*d, ∅ing, r, s*
useful	*ly, ness*
useless	*ly, ness*
usher	*ed, ing, s*
usherette	*s*
usual	*ly, ness*

∅ Drop **e** before adding *ing*

＊　urn
　　earn

ut va   ve

ut

utensil	s
utmost	
utter	ed, ing, ance, s
utter	ly, most, ness

va

vacanc y	ies
vacant	ly
vacate	d, ǿing, s
vacation	s
vaccinate	d, ǿing, s
vacuum	-cleaner, -flask, s
vague	r, st, ly, ness
vain* (proud)	er, est, ly
vale* (valley)	s
valentine	s
valiant	ly
valley	s
valuable	s
value	d, ǿing, less, r, s
valve	s
vane* (weathercock)	s
vanilla	
vanish	ed, ing, es
vanit y	ies
vanquish	ed, ing, es
variet y	ies
various	ly, ness
varnish	ed, ing, es
vary	ing
var ied	ies
vase	s
vaseline	
vast	er, est, ly, ness
vault	ed, ing, er, s

ve

veal	
vegetable	s
vegetarian	s
vegetation	
vehicle	s
veil* (a covering)	ed, ing, s
vein* (blood-vessel)	ed, ing, s
velvet	y, s
vengeance	
venison	
vent	ed, ing, -hole, s
ventilate	d, ǿing, s
ventilation	
ventilator	s
ventriloquist	s
venture	d, ǿing, some, s
veranda(h)	s
verb	al, ally, s
verdict	s
verge	d, ǿing, s
verger	s
vermilion	s
vermin	ous, ously
verse	s
version	s
versus	
vertical	ly
very	
vessel	s
vest	s
vestibule	s
vestr y	ies
vet	ted, ting, s
veteran	s
veterinar y	ies
vex	ed, ing, es, ation, atious

ǿ Drop **e** before adding *ing*

*	vain	vale
	vane	veil
	vein	

vi   vo vu wa

vi

viaduct	s
vibrate	d, ∉ing, s
vibration	s
vicar	age, s
vice	-admiral, -captain, s
vicious	ly, ness
victim	s
victor	s
victorious	ly, ness
victory	ies
victual	led, ling, ler, s
videotape	d, ∉ing, s
view	ed, ing, er, point, s
vigorous	ly, ness
vigour	
viking	s
vile	r, st, ly, ness
villa	s
village	r, s
villain* (scoundrel)	ous, ously, s
villein* (serf)	s
vine	yard, s
vinegar	y
violence	
violent	ly
violet	s
violin	ist, s
virtue	s
visible	y
visibility	
vision	s
visit	ed, ing, or, s
vital	ity, ly
vivarium	s or **vivaria**
vivid	ly, ness
vixen	s

vo

vocabulary	ies
vocalist	s
voice	d, ∉ing, s
volcano	es
vole	s
volley	ēd, ing, -ball, s
volt	age, s
volume	s
voluntary	ily
volunteer	ed, ing, s
vomit	ed, ing, s
vote	d, ∉ing, r, s
vouch	ed, ing, es
voucher	s
vow	ed, ing, s
vowel	s
voyage	d, ∉ing, r, s

vu

vulgar	ity, ly
vulnerable	ness
vulture	s

wa

waddle	d, ∉ing, r, s
wade	d, ∉ing, r, s
wafer	s
waft	ed, ing, er, s
wag	ged, ging, ger, s
wage	d, ∉ing, r, -earner, s
waggle	d, ∉ing, r, s
wagon or **waggon**	er, -load, s
waif	s
wail	ed, ing, er, s

∉ Drop **e** before adding *ing*

* villain
  villein

we

waist* (of body)	*coat, s*
wait* (stay; serve)	*ed, ing, s*
waiter	*s*
waitress	*es*
waiting-room	*s*
wake	*d, ẹing, r, s*
waken	*ed, ing, er, s*
walk	*ed, ing, er, s*
walking-stick	*s*
wall	*ed, ing, chart, flower, paper, s*
wallet	*s*
wallow	*ed, ing, er, s*
walnut	*-tree, s*
walrus	*es*
waltz	*ed, ing, es*
wand	*s*
wander	*ed, ing, er, s*
wangle	*d, ẹing, r, s*
want	*ed, ing, s*
war*	*-dance, -paint, -path, ship, s*
war-cry	*ies*
warrior	*s*
warble	*d, ẹing, r, s*
ward	*ed, ing, en, er, s*
wardrobe	*s*
ware* (goods)	*house, s*
warm	*th, ed, ing, er, est, ish, ly, s*
warn* (be careful)	*ed, ing, er, s*
warp	*ed, ing, s*
warrant	*ed, ing, s*
warren	*s*
wart	*s*
wary	*ier, iest, ily, iness*
wash	*able, ed, ing, es*
washer	*s*
wasn't (was not)	
wasp	*s*

waste*	*d, ẹing, land, -bin, -paper, -pipe, s*
wasteful	*ly, ness*
watch	*ed, ing, man, men, es*
watchful	*ly, ness*
water	*ed, ing, -colour, cress, fall, proof, s*
water-lily	*ies*
watery	*ier, iest, ily, iness*
wave	*d, ẹing, s*
waver	*ed, ing, er, s*
wavy	*ier, iest, ily, iness*
wax	*ed, ing, en, es, works*
waxy	*ier, iest, ily, iness*
way* (direction; manner; road)	*lay, side, s*

we

weak* (not strong)	*er, est, ly, ness, -kneed*
weaken	*ed, ing, s*
weakling	*s*
wealth	
wealthy	*ier, iest, ily, iness*
weapon	*s*
wear* (dressed in)	*ing, er, s*
weary	*ing*
wearied	*ier, iest, ily, iness, ies*
weasel	*s*
weather*	*ed, ing, cock, -forecast, -vane, s*
weave	*d, ẹing, r, s*
we'd (we had; we should; we would)	
wed	*ded, ding, s*
wedding	*-cake, -card, -day, -ring, -bell, s*
wedding-dress	*es*
wedge	*d, ẹing, s*
Wednesday	*s*
weed	*ed, ing, er, -killer, s*
weedy	*ier, iest, iness*
week* (seven days)	*-day, -end, s*

*ẹ Drop **e** before adding ing*

waist	wait	war	ware	warn	way	weak	weather
waste	weight	wore	wear	worn	weigh	week	whether

wh

weekl y			*ies*
weep		*ing, y, er, s*	
wept			
weigh* (measure heaviness)		*ed, ing, s*	
weight* (heaviness)		*ed, ing, -lifter, s*	
weight y	*ier, iest, ily, iness*		
weir			*s*
weird	*er, est, ly, ness*		
welcome		*d, ɇing, s*	
weld		*ed, ing, er, s*	
welfare			
well	*-behaved, -bred, -wisher, s*		
we'll (we shall; we will)			
wellington boot			*s*
went			
wept			
we're (we are)			
were			
weren't (were not)			
west	*ern, erly, ward, wards*		
wet	*ted, ting, ter, test, ly, ness, s*		
we've (we have)			

wh

whack		*ed, ing, s*
whale	*ɇing, r, bone, -boat, s*	
wharf	*s* or **wharves**	
what		*ever, soever*
what's (what is)		
wheat	*-field, -flour, germ, s*	
wheedle		*d, ɇing, r, s*
wheel	*ed, ing, er, barrow, -chair, s*	
wheeze		*d, ɇing, s*
whelk		*s*
when		*ever*
whence		

where	*abouts, as, by, fore, upon*
wherever	
whether* (if)	
which* (what one? who?)	*ever*
whiff	*ed, ing, s*
while	*d, ɇing, s*
whilst	
whimper	*ed, ing, er, s*
whine* (cry; wail)	*d, ɇing, r, s*
whip	*ped, ping, per, s*
whippet	*s*
whirl	*ed, ing, igig, pool, wind, s*
whisk	*ed, ing, er, s*
whisker	*ed, y, s*
whisk y	*ies*
whisper	*ed, ing, er, s*
whist	*-drive*
whistle	*d, ɇing, r, s*
white	*r, st, ly, ness, s*
whiten	*ed, ing, er, s*
whitewash	*ed, ing, es*
whiting	*s* or **whiting**
Whit Sunday	*s*
Whitsun	*tide*
whiz *zes* or **whizz**	*ed, ing, es*
who	*ever*
who'd (who had; who would)	
who'll (who will; who shall)	
who're (who are)	
who's* (who is)	
whom	*soever*
whole* (all; complete)	*sale, some*
wholly* (completely)	
whoop	*ed, ing, s*
whortleberr y	*ies*
whose* (belonging to whom)	
why	

ɇ Drop **e** before adding *ing*

* weigh	weight	whether	which	whine	who's	whole	wholly
way	wait	weather	witch	wine	whose	hole	holy

wi   wo

wi		**wise**	r, st, ly
wicked	er, est, ly, ness	**wish**	ed, ing, es
wicker	work	**wishful**	ly, ness
wicket	-keeper, s	**wistful**	ly, ness
wide	r, st, ly, spread, s	**wit**	ted, less, s
widen	ed, ing, er, s	**witt** y	ier, iest, ily, iness
width	s	**witch*** (old woman)	es, craft, -hunt
widow	ed, ing, er, s	**with**	in, out
wield	ed, ing, er, s	**withdraw**	al, ing, n, s
wife	ly, **wives**	**withdrew**	
wiggle	d, ǿing, r, s	**wither**	ed, ing, s
wigwam	s	**withstand**	ing, s
wild	er, est, ly, ness, life, fowl, fire, s	**withstood**	
wilderness	es	**witness**	ed, ing, -box, es
wilful	ly, ness	**wizard**	ry, s
will	ed, ing, -power, s	**wizened**	
willing	ly, ness		
willow	-herb, -tree, -warbler, s		
wil y	ier, iest, ily, iness	**wo**	
win	ning, ner, s	**wobble**	d, ǿing, r, s
wince	d, ǿing, s	**woe**	begone, s
wind (turn; twist)	ing, er, s	**woeful**	ly, ness
wind	ed, ing, -chart, fall, mill, ward, s	**woke**	n
wind y	ier, iest, ily, iness	**wolf**	-cub, -pack, **wolves**
window	-cleaner, -ledge, -pane, -sill, s	**woman**	hood, ly, **women**
windscreen	-wiper, s	**won*** (win)	
wine* (a drink)	d, ǿing, -bottle, cask, s	**wonder**	ed, ing, ment, land, s
wing	ed, ing, er, -span, s	**wonderful**	ly, ness
wink	ed, ing, er, s	**won't** (will not)	
winkle	d, ǿing, s	**wood***	ed, man, men, -cutter, land, s
winter	ed, ing, -time, s	**wooden**	ly, ness
wintr y	ier, iest, ily, iness	**wood**-louse	-lice
wipe	d, ǿing, r, s	**woodpecker**	s
wire	d, ǿing, -netting, -rope, -cutter, s	**woodwork**	
wireless	ed, ing, es	**wool**	s
wir y	ier, iest, ily, iness	**woollen**	s
wisdom	-tooth, -teeth	**wooll** y	ier, iest, iness, ies

ǿ Drop **e** before adding *ing*

wr   x ya ye

word	*ed, ing, s*
wore* (wear)	
work	*ed, ing, man, men, shop, er, s*
world	*-famous, -wide, s*
worm	*ed, ing, y, eaten, -cast, -hole, s*
worn* (wear)	*-out*
worry	*ing*
worr*ied*	*ier, ies, isome*
worse	
worsen	*ed, ing, s*
worst	
worship	*ped, ping, per, s*
worth	*while*
worthless	*ly, ness*
worth*y*	*ier, iest, ily, iness, ies*
would* (past of will)	
wouldn't (would not)	
wound (turned; twisted)	
wound (injure)	*ed, ing, s*
wove	*n*

wr

wrangle	*d, ☙ing, r, s*
wrap* (cover)	*ped, ping, per, s*
wrath	*ful, fully*
wreath	*s*
wreck	*age, ed, ing, er, s*
wren	*s*
wrench	*ed, ing, es*
wrestle	*d, ☙ing, r, s*
wretch	*es*
wretched	*ly, ness*
wriggle	*d, ☙ing, r, s*
wring* (twist)	*ing, er, s*
wrinkle	*d, ☙ing, r, s*
wrist	*let, band, s*

write* (form letters)	*r, s*
writing	*-case, -desk, -paper, -table, s*
written	
writhe	*d, ☙ing, s*
wrong	*ed, ing, ful, ly, ness, s*
wrote	
wrung* (twisted)	
wry	*er, est, ly, ness*

x

X-ray	*ed, ing, s*
xylophone	*s*

ya

yacht	*ing, sman, smen, -club, s*
yak	*s*
yap	*ped, ping, per, s*
yard	*age, stick, s*
yarn	*ed, ing, s*
yawn	*ed, ing, s*

ye

year	*ly, ling, s*
yearn	*ed, ing, s*
yeast	*y*
yell	*ed, ing, er, s*
yellow	*er, est, ness, ish, y, s*
yelp	*ed, ing, er, s*
yeo*man*	*men*
yes	*es*
yesterday	*s*
yet	
yeti	*s*
yew*	*-tree, s*

*☙ Drop **e** before adding* ing

*	wore	worn	would	wrap	wring	write	wrung	yew
	war	warn	wood	rap	ring	right	rung	you
								ewe

yi yu yo ze zi zo zu

yi
yield	*ed, ing, s*

yo
yodel	*led, ling, ler, s*
yoga	
yog(h)urt	
yoke* (wooden bar; join)	*d, eing, s*
yokel	*s*
yolk* (of egg)	*s*
yonder	
Yorkshire pudding	*s*
you* (person)	
you'd (you had; you would)	
you'll (you will)	
you're (you are)	
you've (you have)	
young	*er, est, ish*
youngster	*s*
your	
yours	
your *self*	*selves*
youth	*-club, s*
youthful	*ly, ness*
yowl	*ed, ing, er, s*

yu
yule	*-log, tide, s*

ze
zeal	
zealous	*ly*
zebra	*s*
zebu	*s*
zephyr	*s*
zero	*s*
zest	*ful, fully*

zi
zigzag	*ged, ging, s*
zinc	
zip	*ped, ping, per, -fastener, s*
zither	*s*

zo
zodiac	
zone	*d, eing, s*
zoo	*s*
zoological garden	*s*
zoologist	*s*
zoology	
zoom	*ed, ing, s*

zu
Zulu	*s*

*e Drop **e** before adding ing*

*	yoke	you
	yolk	yew
		ewe

Boys' Names

A
Aaron
Adam
Adrian
Alan
Alexander
Alistair
Alfred
Allan
Andrew
Angus
Anthony
Antony
Arthur
Ashley

B
Barry
Benjamin
Bernard
Brendan
Brian
Bryan
Bruce

C
Calvin
Carl
Cedric
Charles
Christian
Christopher
Clifford
Clive
Colin
Courtenay
Craig

D
Dale
Damian
Daniel
Darren
David
Dean
Dennis
Derek
Dominic
Donald
Duncan
Dylan

E
Edmund
Edward
Eric

F
Francis
Frank
Frederick

G
Gareth
Gary
Gavin
Geoffrey
George
Giles
Glen(n)
Glyn
Gordon
Graham
Gregory
Guy

H
Henry
Howard
Hugh

I
Ian
Ivan

J
James
Jamie
Jason
Jeffrey
Jeremy
Jocelyn
John
Jonathan
Joseph
Julian
Justin

K
Karl
Keith
Kenneth
Kevin

L
Lance
Laurence
Lawrence
Lee
Leon
Leonard
Leslie
Luke

M
Malcolm
Marc
Marcus
Mark
Martin
Martyn
Matthew
Maurice
Melvin
Mervyn
Michael
Miles

N
Nathan
Nathaniel
Neil
Neville
Nicholas
Nigel
Noel
Norman

O
Oliver
Owen

P
Patrick
Paul
Peter
Philip
Piers

Q
Quentin

R
Ralph
Randolph
Raymond
Reginald
Rex
Richard
Robert
Robin
Roderick
Rodney
Roger
Roland
Rolf
Ronald
Roy
Royston
Rufus
Rupert
Russell
Ryan

S
Samuel
Scott
Sebastian
Seán
Shane
Shaun
Sidney
Simon
Spencer
Stanley
Stephen
Steven
Stewart
Stuart

T
Terence
Terry
Thomas
Timothy
Tony
Trevor
Tristram

V
Vernon
Victor
Vincent
Vivian

W
Wallace
Walter
Warren
Wayne
Wilfred
William
Winston

Girls' Names

A
Abigail
Adele
Adrienne
Aileen
Alexandra
Alexis
Alice
Alison
Amanda
Amelia
Amy
Andrea
Angela
Anita
Ann(e)
Anna
Annabel
Annabella
Annette
Anthea
Antonia
April
Audra
Audrey
Averil

B
Barbara
Belinda
Beryl
Betty
Beverley
Blanche
Brenda
Bridget
Bryony

C
Cara
Carla
Carol(e)
Caroline
Carolyn
Carrie
Catherine
Cecilia
Celia
Charlotte
Charmaine
Cheryl
Chloe
Christine
Claire
Clare
Claudia
Colette
Corinne

D
Danielle
Daphne
Dawn
Debbie
Deborah
Debra
Deirdre
Delia
Della
Denise
Diana
Diane
Dionne
Donna
Dorothy

E
Eileen
Elaine
Eleanor
Elizabeth
Ellen
Emily
Emma
Enid
Erica
Esmé(e)
Estelle
Ester
Eveline
Evelyn

F
Fay(e)
Felicity
Fiona
Fleur
Frances

G
Gabrielle
Gail
Gayle
Gaynor
Gemma
Georgina
Geraldine
Germaine
Gillian
Gina
Glenda
Glynis
Gwyneth

H
Hannah
Hayley
Hazel
Heather
Heidi
Helen
Hilary
Holly

I
Irene
Isabel

J
Jacqueline
Jane
Janet
Janice
Janine
Jayne
Jean
Jeanette
Jennifer
Jessica
Jill
Joan
Joanna
Joanne
Johanna
Josephine
Joy
Judith
Julia
Julie
June
Justine

K
Karen
Kate
Katharine
Katherine
Kathleen
Kathryn
Katrina
Kay
Keeley
Kelly
Kerry
Kimberly
Kitty
Kirsten
Kirsty

L
Laura
Leanne
Lesley
Linda
Lindsey
Lisa
Lorna
Lorraine
Louisa
Louise
Lucy
Lyndsey
Lynn(e)

M
Madeleine
Mandy
Margaret
Maria

Marie
Martina
Mary
Matilda
Maureen
Maxine
Melanie
Melinda
Melissa
Merle
Michelle
Miranda

N
Nadia
Nadine
Nancy
Naomi
Natalie
Natasha
Nichola
Nicola
Nicole
Nina

O
Olivia

P
Pamela
Patricia
Paula
Pauline
Penelope
Penny
Philippa
Polly

R
Rachael
Rachel
Rebecca
Rebekah
Rita
Rosalie
Rosalind
Rosamund
Rose
Rosemary
Rowena
Ruth

S
Sadie
Sally
Sallyann
Samantha
Sandra
Sara(h)
Sharon
Sheila
Shelley
Shirley
Shona
Sonia
Sophie
Stacey
Stella
Stephanie
Susan
Susannah
Susanne
Suzanne
Sybil
Sylvia

T
Tamara
Tammy
Tamsin
Tania
Tanya
Tara
Teresa
Theresa
Tina
Tracey
Tracy

U
Ursula

V
Valerie
Vanessa
Vicki
Vicky
Victoria
Virginia
Vivien
Vivienne

W
Wendy

Y
Yolande
Yvonne

Z
Zara
Zelda
Zoe

Numbers

Cardinal		Ordinal			Roman
1	one _s_	first	_ly, s_	1st	I
2	two _s_	second	_ly, s_	2nd	II
3	three _s_	third	_ly, s_	3rd	III
4	four _s_	fourth	_ly, s_	4th	IV
5	five _s_	fifth	_ly, s_	5th	V
6	six _es_	sixth	_ly, s_	6th	VI
7	seven _s_	seventh	_ly, s_	7th	VII
8	eight _s_	eighth	_ly, s_	8th	VIII
9	nine _s_	ninth	_ly, s_	9th	IX
10	ten _s_	tenth	_ly, s_	10th	X
11	eleven _s_	eleventh	_s_	11th	XI
12	twelve _s_	twelfth	_s_	12th	XII
13	thirteen _s_	thirteenth	_s_	13th	XIII
14	fourteen _s_	fourteenth	_s_	14th	XIV
15	fifteen _s_	fifteenth	_s_	15th	XV
16	sixteen _s_	sixteenth	_s_	16th	XVI
17	seventeen _s_	seventeenth	_s_	17th	XVII
18	eighteen _s_	eighteenth	_s_	18th	XVIII
19	nineteen _s_	nineteenth	_s_	19th	XIX
20	twent_y_ _ies_	twentieth	_s_	20th	XX
21	twenty-one _s_	twenty-first	_s_	21st	XXI
22	twenty-two _s_	twenty-second	_s_	22nd	XXII
23	twenty-three _s_	twenty-third	_s_	23rd	XXIII
24	twenty-four _s_	twenty-fourth	_s_	24th	XXIV
25	twenty-five _s_	twenty-fifth	_s_	25th	XXV
26	twenty-six _es_	twenty-sixth	_s_	26th	XXVI
27	twenty-seven _s_	twenty-seventh	_s_	27th	XXVII
28	twenty-eight _s_	twenty-eighth	_s_	28th	XXVIII
29	twenty-nine _s_	twenty-ninth	_s_	29th	XXIX
30	thirt_y_ _ies_	thirtieth	_s_	30th	XXX
31	thirty-one _s_	thirty-first	_s_	31st	XXXI
40	fort_y_ _ies_	fortieth	_s_	40th	XL
41	forty-one _s_	forty-first	_s_	41st	XLI

	Cardinal		Ordinal			Roman
50	fift*y*	*ies*	fiftieth	*s*	50th	L
51	fifty-one	*s*	fifty-first	*s*	51st	LI
60	sixt*y*	*ies*	sixtieth	*s*	60th	LX
61	sixty-one	*s*	sixty-first	*s*	61st	LXI
70	sevent*y*	*ies*	seventieth	*s*	70th	LXX
71	seventy-one	*s*	seventy-first	*s*	71st	LXXI
80	eight*y*	*ies*	eightieth	*s*	80th	LXXX
81	eighty-one	*s*	eighty-first	*s*	81st	LXXXI
90	ninet*y*	*ies*	ninetieth	*s*	90th	XC
91	ninety-one	*s*	ninety-first	*s*	91st	XCI
100	hundred	*s*	hundredth	*s*	100th	C
500	five hundred		five hundreth		500th	D
1,000	thousand	*s*	thousandth	*s*	1,000th	M
10,000	ten thousand		ten thousandth		10,000th	
100,000	one hundred thousand		one hundred thousandth		100,000th	
1,000,000	million	*s*	millionth	*s*	1,000,000th	

Roman numerals

When a smaller number comes *before* a larger one, it is subtracted,
e.g. IV = 5 − 1 = 4; IX = 10 − 1 = 9; XL = 50 − 10 = 40; CD = 500 − 100 = 400

When a smaller number comes *after* a larger one, it is added,
e.g. VI = 5 + 1 = 6; XI = 10 + 1 = 11; LX = 50 + 10 = 60; DC = 500 + 100 = 600

Countries and Peoples of the World

Afghanistan	Afghan	s
Albania	Albanian	s
Algeria	Algerian	s
America (see United States of America)		
Angola	Angolan	s
Argentina	Argentinian	s
Australia	Australian	s
Austria	Austrian	s
Bangladesh	Bangladeshi	s
Belarus (see Belorussia)		
Belgium	Belgian	s
Belorussia	Belorussian	s
Benin	Beninese	
Bhutan	Bhutanese	
Bolivia	Bolivian	s
Botswana	Citizen of Botswana	
Brazil	Brazilian	s
Britain	British (plural) or Briton	s
Bulgaria	Bulgarian	s
Burma (now called Myanmar)	Burmese	
Cambodia	Cambodian	s
Cameroon	Cameroonian	s
Canada	Canadian	s
Central African Republic	Person of the Central African Republic	
Chad	Chadian	s
Chile	Chilean	s
China	Chinese	
Colombia	Colombian	s
Congo	Congolese	
Costa Rica	Costa Rican	s
Cuba	Cuban	s
Cyprus	Cypriot	s
Czech Republic	Czech	s
Denmark	Dane	s

Ecuador	Ecuadorean	s
Egypt	Egyptian	s
England	English (plural)	
Ethiopia	Ethiopian	s
Falkland Islands	Falkland Islander	s
Fiji	Fijian	s
Finland	Finn	s
France	French (plural)	
Gambia	Gambian	s
Germany	German	s
Ghana	Ghanaian	s
Great Britain (see Britain)		
Greece	Greek	s
Guatemala	Guatemalan	s
Guinea	Guinean	s
Guyana	Guyanese	
Haiti	Haitian	s
Holland (see Netherlands)		
Honduras	Honduran	s
Hong Kong	Inhabitant of Hong Kong	
Hungary	Hungarian	s
Iceland	Icelander	s
India	Indian	s
Indonesia	Indonesian	s
Iran	Iranian	s
Iraq	Iraqi	s
Ireland, Republic of	Irish (plural)	
Israel	Israeli	s
Italy	Italian	s
Jamaica	Jamaican	s
Japan	Japanese	
Jordan	Jordanian	s
Kazakhstan	Kazakh	s
Kenya	Kenyan	s
Korea (North, South)	Korean	s

Country	Nationality	s
Kuwait	Kuwaiti	s
Lebanon	Lebanese	
Liberia	Liberian	s
Libya	Libyan	s
Luxembourg	Luxembourger	s
Madagascar	Malagasy *Malagasies*	
Malawi	Malawian	s
Malaysia	Malaysian	s
Mali	Malian	s
Mauritania	Mauritanian	s
Mauritius	Mauritian	s
Mexico	Mexican	s
Moldavia, Moldova	Moldavian	s
Monaco	Monégasque	s
Mongolia	Mongolian	s
Morocco	Moroccan	s
Mozambique	Mozambican	s
Myanmar (until 1989 called *Burma*)		
Namibia	Namibian	s
Nepal	Nepalese	
Netherlands	Dutch *(plural)*	
New Zealand	New Zealander	s
Nicaragua	Nicaraguan	s
Niger	Nigerien	s
Nigeria	Nigerian	s
Norway	Norwegian	s
Oman	Omani	s
Pakistan	Pakistani	s
Panama	Panamanian	s
Papua New Guinea	Papua New Guinean	s
Paraguay	Paraguayan	s
Peru	Peruvian	s
Philippines	Filipino	s
Poland	Pole	s
Portugal	Portuguese	
Romania	Romanian	s
Russia	Russian	s
Saudi Arabia	Saudi Arabian	s
Scotland	Scot	s
Senegal	Senegalese	

Country	Nationality	s
Sierra Leone	Sierra Leonean	s
Singapore	Singaporean	s
Slovakia	Slovak	s
Somalia	Somali	s
South Africa	South African	s
Spain	Spanish *(plural)*, Spaniard	s
Sri Lanka	Sri Lankan	s
Sudan	Sudanese	
Sweden	Swede	s
Switzerland	Swiss	
Syria	Syrian	s
Tanzania	Tanzanian	s
Thailand	Thai	s
Trinidad and Tobago	Trinidadian and Tobagan or Tobagonian	s
Tunisia	Tunisian	s
Turkey	Turk	s
Uganda	Ugandan	s
Ukraine	Ukrainian	s
Union of Soviet Socialist Republics (until 1991)	Russian	s
United Arab Emirates	Person of the United Arab Emirates	
United Kingdom	British *(plural)*	
United States of America	American	s
Uruguay	Uruguayan	s
Uzbekistan	Uzbek	s
Venezuela	Venezuelan	s
Vietnam	Vietnamese	
Wales	Welsh *(plural)*	
Yemen, Republic of	Yemeni	s
Zaïre	Zaïrean	s
Zambia	Zambian	s
Zimbabwe	Zimbabwean	s

Parts of Speech

Noun: A naming word, e.g. *boy, man, cat, house, Susan, England*.
On *Monday John* went by *coach* to *London Zoo* with his
teacher, Mr. Smith, and other *children* from his *class*.

Pronoun: A word used instead of a noun, e.g. *me, she, it, we, us, him*.
You and *I* will go now and *he* can come later with *them*.

Adjective: A word that is 'added to' a noun to describe it, e.g.
fat, thin, big, brown, green, ugly, pretty, delicious.
A *funny, little, old* man with a *large* nose and a *grey*
beard showed the *small* children his *beautiful* garden.

Verb: A doing word; a word that tells what is done, e.g.
do, go, stay, talk, shout, jump, lift, fight, eat, drink.
Stop running or you will *fall* and *hurt* yourself.

Adverb: A word that tells how, when or where something happens, e.g.
soon, often, there, now, never, quickly, carefully, carelessly.
Yesterday when I came *here* I jumped *over* that wall.

Preposition: A word that is placed before a noun, e.g.
by, in, into, at, for, under, over, against, near.
Bob went *with* his sister *on* a bus *to* the town.

Conjunction: A word that joins sentences, phrases or words, e.g.
or, than, though, although, because, while, unless.
John *and* Mary will go *if* it is fine *but* not *if* it rains.

Interjection: A word used as an exclamation, e.g. *Ah! Alas! Hey!*
Oh! You did frighten me. *Ouch!* That hurt.

Article: One of the three words – *a, an* or *the*.
A boy rode on *an* elephant at *the* zoo.

Spelling Lists of Words to Learn

The following lists contain the words you will need to use most often in your writing and compositions. You should, therefore, learn and try to remember how to spell all these words. Choose the shortest and easiest words at the beginning of each section to learn first. It is better to learn a few words each day rather than a long list, at one time, once a week. To make it easier for you the words are usually arranged in lists according to the number of letters in the words: three, four, five letters, etc. The number at the top of a word list shows the number of letters in each word in that list. Before you start to learn a list of words first study all the words in the list and notice that some words have the same letters in exactly the same order as others in the list.

All the words on pages 118 to 123 and at the bottom of page 126 are verbs, or may be used as verbs, and are arranged in lists according to the way in which their *ed, ing, s* endings are formed. When your teacher tests you on the words you have learnt he/she will probably ask you how to spell some of these words with their *ed, ing, s* endings to see whether you have understood this, e.g.

bark	**scare**	**drop**
mark *ed*	**score** *d*	**chop** *ped*
park *ing*	**stor** *ing*	**shop** *ping*
work *s*	**stone** *s*	**stop** *s*

You may add *ed, ing, s* to all the following words, e.g.
camp *ed, ing, s* = **camped, camping, camps**

3		4		4		4	
act	*ed, ing, s*	**book**	*ed, ing, s*	**back**	*ed, ing, s*	**camp**	*ed, ing, s*
add		**cook**		**pack**		**damp**	
air		**hook**		**sack**		**bump**	
arm		**look**		**dock**		**dump**	
ask		**cool**		**lock**		**jump**	
end		**pool**		**rock**		**lump**	
ink		**show**		**kick**		**pump**	
oil		**slow**		**lick**		**bomb**	
own		**flow**		**pick**		**comb**	
toy		**snow**		**tick**		**lamb**	

4		4		4		4	
dust	*ed, ing, s*	**call**	*ed, ing, s*	**bark**	*ed, ing, s*	**load**	*ed, ing, s*
last		**fell**		**mark**		**boat**	
list		**well**		**park**		**coat**	
nest		**yell**		**work**		**roar**	
rest		**fill**		**cork**		**soap**	
test		**kill**		**fork**		**help**	
post		**mill**		**milk**		**long**	
lift		**will**		**talk**		**hunt**	
melt		**pull**		**walk**		**want**	
salt		**roll**		**bank**		**word**	

4		4		4		4	
form	*ed, ing, s*	**gain**	*ed, ing, s*	**head**	*ed, ing, s*	**bath**	*ed, ing, s*
farm		**pain**		**heal**		**down**	
harm		**rain**		**heat**		**even**	
warm		**pair**		**seat**		**open**	
band		**fail**		**fear**		**turn**	
hand		**jail**		**near**		**join**	
land		**nail**		**team**		**iron**	
sand		**sail**		**play**		**part**	
bang		**tail**		**pray**		**mind**	
gang		**wait**		**stay**		**view**	

5		5		5		6	
clean	ed, ing, s	knock	ed, ing, s	thank	ed, ing, s	answer	ed, ing, s
clear		clock		train		corner	
climb		block		tramp		flower	
cloud		shock		treat		bother	
clown		black		light		gather	
chain		crack		right		matter	
chair		track		sight		master	
chalk		brick		dream		murder	
cheer		trick		radio		number	
cheat		wreck		visit		wonder	

5		5		6		6	
enter	ed, ing, s	count	ed, ing, s	appear	ed, ing, s	remind	ed, ing, s
cover		cough		arrest		return	
lower		rough		attack		reward	
offer		round		happen		school	
order		pound		hollow		scream	
water		sound		follow		stream	
paper		mouth		borrow		belong	
paint		group		button		poison	
point		scout		butter		powder	
plant		shout		letter		obtain	

5		5		6		7	
laugh	ed, ing, s	boast	ed, ing, s	colour	ed, ing, s	explain	ed, ing, s
haunt		coast		doctor		contain	
field		roast		ground		curtain	
float		toast		garden		captain	
floor		start		awaken		holiday	
flood		stamp		fasten		journey	
bloom		storm		listen		present	
stoop		allow		pocket		pretend	
spoon		enjoy		rocket		soldier	
sport		guard		ticket		station	

5		6+		6+		7+	
crawl	ed, ing, s	expect	ed, ing, s	repair	ed, ing, s	disobey	ed, ing, s
creak		collect		remain		discover	
crowd		correct		remind		disappear	
crown		protect		remember		disappoint	

You may add *ing* and *s* to the following words. You may not add *ed*. The words on the right of the columns are used instead.

buy	*ing, s* : **bought**	wear	*ing, s* : **wore, worn**
lay	: **laid**	ring	: **rang, rung**
pay	: **paid**	sing	: **sang, sung**
say	: **said**	spring	: **sprang, sprung**
cost	: **cost**	sink	: **sank, sunk**
feed	: **fed**	drink	: **drank, drunk**
feel	: **felt**	think	: **thought**
find	: **found**	bring	: **brought**
hear	: **heard**	fight	: **fought**
hold	: **held**	build	: **built**
hurt	*ing, s* : **hurt**	shoot	*ing, s* : **shot**
keep	: **kept**	sleep	: **slept**
lead	: **led**	stand	: **stood**
lend	: **lent**	spend	: **spent**
send	: **sent**	sweep	: **swept**
sell	: **sold**	swing	: **swung**
tell	: **told**	spread	: **spread**
meet	: **met**	break	: **broke,** *n*
mean	: **meant**	speak	: **spoke,** *n*
read	: **read**	steal	: **stole,** *n*
see	*n, ing, s* : **saw**	eat	*en, ing, s* : **ate**
blow	*n, ing, s* : **blew**	beat	*en, ing, s* : **beat**
draw	*n, ing, s* : **drew**	fall	*en, ing, s* : **fell**
grow	*n, ing, s* : **grew**		
know	*n, ing, s* : **knew**	catch	*ing, es* : **caught**
throw	*n, ing, s* : **threw**	teach	*ing, es* : **taught**

You may add *ed*, *ing*, *es* to all the following words:

box *ed, ing, es*	fish *ed, ing, es*	kiss *ed, ing, es*	fetch *ed, ing, es*
fix	dish	miss	match
mix	push	cross	watch
	rush	pass	scratch
	wash	class	march
	wish	grass	reach
	brush	guess	bunch
	crash	press	lunch
	flash	dress	touch
	finish	address	search

All the following words end in a consonant followed by a letter **e**.
You may add *d* and *s* to all the words but the **e** must be dropped before adding *ing*, e.g.

      hope *d, ̷eing, s* = **hoped, hoping, hopes**

4		4		4		5	
care *d, ̷eing, s*		dive *d, ̷eing, s*		hope *d, ̷eing, s*		argue *d, ̷eing, s*	
dare		tire		rope		blame	
face		fire		note		flame	
race		wire		hole		place	
save		wipe		love		dance	
wave		fine		move		piece	
hate		line		name		force	
bake		live		side		voice	
rake		like		time		price	
wake		hike		type		prize	

*ȩ́ Drop **e** before adding *ing*

continued on page 122

5		5		6		6	
chase	*d, ǿing, s*	**scare**	*d, ǿing, s*	**battle**	*d, ǿing, s*	**arrive**	*d, ǿing, s*
close		**score**		**bottle**		**behave**	
cause		**store**		**settle**		**chance**	
pause		**stone**		**bubble**		**bridge**	
house		**smile**		**paddle**		**change**	
amuse		**serve**		**puzzle**		**charge**	
raise		**taste**		**bundle**		**garage**	
nurse		**waste**		**double**		**damage**	
sense		**brave**		**hurdle**		**manage**	
tease		**prove**		**single**		**voyage**	

6		7		7		8	
decide	*d, ǿing, s*	**balance**	*d, ǿing, s*	**picture**	*d, ǿing, s*	**surprise**	*d, ǿing, s*
divide		**bandage**		**promise**		**exercise**	
invite		**believe**		**provide**		**exchange**	
escape		**bicycle**		**prepare**		**celebrate**	
notice		**breathe**		**produce**		**continue**	
excuse		**deserve**		**grumble**		**decorate**	
refuse		**capture**		**stumble**		**describe**	
rescue		**explore**		**tremble**		**puncture**	
circle		**imagine**		**trouble**		**struggle**	
centre		**receive**		**whistle**		**treasure**	

All the words in the left-hand columns end in a consonant followed by a letter **e**. You may add *s* to all the words but the **e** must be dropped before adding *ing*.

You may not add *d*. The words on the right of the column are used instead.

come	*ǿing, s* : **came**	**bite**	*ǿing, s* : **bit, bitten**
make	: **made**	**hide**	: **hid, hidden**
lose	: **lost**	**ride**	: **rode, ridden**
leave	: **left**	**rise**	: **rose, risen**
slide	: **slid**	**drive**	: **drove, driven**
strike	: **struck**	**write**	: **wrote, written**
		choose	: **chose,** *n*

give	*n, ǿing, s* : **gave**
take	*n, ǿing, s* : **took**
shake	*n, ǿing, s* : **shook**
mistake	*n, ǿing, s* : **mistook**

ǿ Drop **e** before adding *ing*

You may add *s* to all the following words. The final consonant (the last letter) must be doubled before adding *ed, ing,* e.g.

    drop   *ped, ping, s* = **dropped, dropping, drops**

3		3		3		4	
bat	*ted, ting, s*	**dip**	*ped, ping, s*	**beg**	*ged, ging, s*	**drop**	*ped, ping, s*
pat		**rip**		**peg**		**chop**	
pet		**tip**		**gag**		**shop**	
net		**zip**		**wag**		**stop**	
wet		**hop**		**hug**		**swop**	
fit		**pop**		**tug**		**ship**	
rot		**top**		**gun**		**slip**	
rob		**tap**		**sun**		**skip**	
mob		**map**		**pin**		**drip**	
sob		**yap**		**jab**		**grip**	

4		4		5+		5+	
trip	*ped, ping, s*	**plan**	*ned, ning, s*	**equal**	*led, ling, s*	**admit**	*ted, ting, s*
whip		**stun**		**signal**		**permit**	
clap		**grin**		**pencil**		**commit**	
snap		**skin**		**model**		**regret**	
trap		**skid**		**cancel**		**occur**	
wrap		**chat**		**parcel**		**refer**	
step		**plot**		**shovel**		**prefer**	
stab		**knot**		**travel**		**equip**	
grab		**knit**		**tunnel**		**kidnap**	
drag		**dial**		**quarrel**		**unwrap**	

None of the following words may end in *ed.*
The words in the right hand column are used instead.

get	*ting, s* : **got**		**dig**	*ging, s* : **dug**	
set	*ting, s* : **set**		**run**	*ning, s* : **ran**	
sit	*ting, s* : **sat**		**win**	*ning, s* : **won**	
hit	*ting, s* : **hit**		**spin**	*ning, s* : **spun**	
cut	*ting, s* : **cut**		**begin**	*ning, s* : **began, begun**	
shut	*ting, s* : **shut**		**swim**	*ming, s* : **swam, swum**	

You may add *er, est, ly, ness* to all the following words, e.g.
bold *er, est, ly, ness* = **bolder**, **boldest**, **boldly**, **boldness**

4		4+		5	
bold	*er, est, ly, ness*	**fair**	*er, est, ly, ness*	**light**	*er, est, ly, ness*
cold		**dear**		**tight**	
poor		**near**		**quick**	
cool		**neat**		**quiet**	
deep		**mean**		**queer**	
dark		**weak**		**steep**	
kind		**clean**		**sharp**	
loud		**clear**		**short**	
rich		**cheap**		**smart**	
slow		**great**		**thick**	
soft		**fresh**		**rough**	
wild		**clever**		**tough**	

You may add *r, st, ly, ness* to the following words:

4		4+	
late	*r, st, ly, ness*	**rude**	*r, st, ly, ness*
nice		**wide**	
fine		**large**	
safe		**close**	
sore		**fierce**	
sure		**strange**	

You may add *ly, ness* to the following words but
the last letter must be doubled before adding *er, est*.

3		3+	
sad	*der, dest, ly, ness*	**fat**	*ter, test*
mad	*der, dest*	**flat**	*ter, test*
hot	*ter, test*	**thin**	*ner, nest*
fit	*ter, test*		

All the following words end in *y*.
The *y* must be dropped before adding *ier, iest, ily, iness*, e.g.

eas*y*   *ier, iest, ily, iness* = **easier, easiest, easily, easiness**

4+

eas*y*   *ier, iest, ily, iness*
laz*y*
tid*y*
tin*y*
ugl*y*
dirt*y*
empt*y*
heav*y*
juic*y*
luck*y*
nois*y*
rock*y*

5

happ*y*   *ier, iest, ily, iness*
sunn*y*
funn*y*
fuss*y*
mess*y*
mudd*y*
joll*y*
sill*y*
sorr*y*
shak*y*
wear*y*
wind*y*

6

stick*y*   *ier, iest, ily, iness*
trick*y*
shabb*y*
prett*y*
lovel*y*
lonel*y*
sleep*y*
greed*y*
cheek*y*
breez*y*
gloom*y*
storm*y*

6+

hungr*y* *ier, iest, ily, iness*
cloud*y*
clums*y*
chill*y*
kindl*y*
stead*y*
untid*y*
unluck*y*
naught*y*
thirst*y*
health*y*
wealth*y*

4+

bus*y*   *ier, iest, ily*
angr*y*   *ier, iest, ily*
earl*y*   *ier, iest, iness*
sand*y*   *ier, iest, iness*
merr*y*   *ier, iest, ily, iment*

dough	also	Monday	January
cough	always	Tuesday	February
rough	almost	Wednesday	March
tough	although	Thursday	April
enough	already	Friday	May
plough	altogether	Saturday	June
through		Sunday	July
ought	all right		August
bought		spring	September
brought		summer	October
fought		autumn	November
thought		winter	December

All the following words end in **y**.
You may add *ing* but the **y** must be dropped before adding *ied, ies.*

cry	*ing*	**carry**	*ing*	**copy**	*ing*
cr *ied*	*ies*	**carr** *ied*	*ies*	**cop** *ied*	*ies*
dry	*ing*	**marry**	*ing*	**bury**	*ing*
dr *ied*	*ies*	**marr** *ied*	*ies*	**bur** *ied*	*ies*
try	*ing*	**hurry**	*ing*	**tidy**	*ing*
tr *ied*	*ies*	**hurr** *ied*	*ies*	**tid** *ied*	*ies*
fry	*ing*	**worry**	*ing*	**occupy**	*ing*
fr *ied*	*ies*	**worr** *ied*	*ies*	**occup** *ied*	*ies*
spy	*ing*	**empty**	*ing*	**satisfy**	*ing*
sp *ied*	*ies*	**empt** *ied*	*ies*	**satisf** *ied*	*ies*
fly	*ing*	**study**	*ing*	**terrify**	*ing*
fl *ies*		**stud** *ied*	*ies*	**terrif** *ied*	*ies*
flew, flown					

A very few verbs end in **ie**. You may add *d* and *s* but the **ie** must be changed to *y* before adding *ing.*

die	*d, s*	**lie**	*d, s*	**tie**	*d, s*
dy *ing*		**ly** *ing*		**ty** *ing*	

Singular		Plural	Singular	Plural	Singular	Plural
foot		feet	bab y	ies	key	s
goose		geese	lad y	ies	donkey	s
tooth		teeth	bod y	ies	monkey	s
mouse		mice	pon y	ies	valley	s
man		men	cit y	ies	chimney	s
woman		women	arm y	ies	cowboy	s
child		children	nav y	ies	railway	s
			aunt y	ies	gangway	s
life		lives	dadd y	ies	holiday	s
wife		wives	mumm y	ies	birthday	s
knife		knives				
			dais y	ies	zoo	s
leaf		leaves	dair y	ies	piano	s
loaf		loaves	fair y	ies	radio	s
thief		thieves	stor y	ies		
			part y	ies	hero	es
dwarf	s or	dwarves	jell y	ies	cargo	es
scarf	s or	scarves	lorr y	ies	Negro	es
wharf	s or	wharves	pupp y	ies	potato	es
hoof	s or	hooves	hobb y	ies	tomato	es
roof	s		enem y	ies	volcano	es
elf		elves	canar y	ies	bus	es
calf		calves	famil y	ies	glass	es
half		halves	grann y	ies	beach	es
wolf		wolves	cherr y	ies	peach	es
shelf		shelves	countr y	ies	torch	es
			librar y	ies	witch	es
self		selves	factor y	ies	church	es
itself			robber y	ies	circus	es
myself			myster y	ies	princess	es
himself			discover y	ies	sandwich	es
herself						
yourself		yourselves	**every**	body, one, thing, where		
		ourselves	**any**	body, one, thing, where, how, way		
		themselves	**some**	body, one, thing, where, how, times		

4	4	5	4		4		5	
able	than	these	bell	s	bird	s	giant	s
away	that	those	ball	s	desk	s	glove	s
best	then	where	wall	s	lake	s	green	s
born	them	which	hall	s	lawn	s	hedge	s
both	they	while	hill	s	lion	s	horse	s
does	this	whole	cake	s	neck	s	hotel	s
done	true	whose	card	s	nose	s	jewel	s
goes	luck	worse	cart	s	page	s	lemon	s
gone	ever	worst	cave	s	path	s	noise	s
gold	very	worth	case	s	pond	s	ocean	s

4	4	5	4		4		5	
dead	went	could	coal	s	shed	s	other	s
deaf	were	would	goal	s	shoe	s	owner	s
each	what	magic	door	s	sock	s	plate	s
else	when	might	food	s	song	s	fruit	s
just	with	money	moon	s	tent	s	pupil	s
must	clay	music	room	s	town	s	purse	s
much	beef	never	wood	s	tree	s	queen	s
many	pork	pence	wool	s	mile	s	salad	s
more	east	sugar	flag	s	your	s	shirt	s
most	west	ready	frog	s	year	s	snake	s

4	5	5	4		5		5	
from	about	among	game	s	apple	s	stair	s
next	above	below	gate	s	baker	s	stick	s
none	after	blood	gift	s	bread	s	stove	s
only	again	earth	hole	s	beast	s	sword	s
once	ahead	often	home	s	cabin	s	table	s
upon	alone	sorry	hour	s	cloth	s	thing	s
same	along	sheep	king	s	comic	s	tiger	s
some	alike	shall	kite	s	dozen	s	truck	s
soon	alive	under	knee	s	front	s	white	s
such	aside	until	idea	s	ghost	s	world	s

6	7	6		6		9	
across	against	friend	s	infant	s	adventure	s
afraid	another	forest	s	insect	s	aeroplane	s
around	because	finger	s	inside	s	afternoon	s
asleep	beneath	father	s	island	s	chocolate	s
ashore	between	mother	s	desert	s	favourite	s
awhile	clothes	leader	s	orange	s	passenger	s
before	instead	reader	s	second	s	newspaper	s
behind	nothing	saucer	s	minute	s	orchestra	s
better	perhaps	sister	s	moment	s	programme	s
cattle	without	reason	s	museum	s	vegetable	s

6	8	6		7		full	y
during	together	bullet	s	bedroom	s	awful	ly
either	tomorrow	carrot	s	blanket	s	useful	ly
famous	horrible	coffee	s	brother	s	careful	ly
hardly	horribly	cotton	s	teacher	s	playful	ly
little	terrible	dinner	s	sausage	s	cheerful	ly
middle	terribly	kitten	s	cabbage	s	dreadful	ly
modern	possible	lesson	s	cottage	s	thankful	ly
unless	possibly	rabbit	s	message	s	beautiful	ly
utmost	probable	robber	s	village	s	forgetful	ly
within	probably	rubber	s	lettuce	s	wonderful	ly

6	6		6		7		helpful	ly
people	animal	s	parent	s	chicken	s	hopeful	ly
petrol	banana	s	person	s	kitchen	s	skilful	ly
plenty	beside	s	prince	s	husband	s	faithful	ly
police	bucket	s	secret	s	pudding	s	grateful	ly
rather	castle	s	street	s	morning	s	peaceful	ly
really	cousin	s	string	s	evening	s	powerful	ly
safety	coward	s	violin	s	tadpole	s	spiteful	ly
should	danger	s	window	s	tractor	s	delightful	ly
seldom	engine	s	pillow	s	visitor	s	disgraceful	ly
silver	needle	s	yellow	s	outside	s		

Contractions *(shortened words)*

These are words which have been shortened by joining two words together and placing an apostrophe where a letter or letters have been left out. Learn the words and the contractions, being very careful to remember exactly where the apostrophe goes.

can't = cannot
don't = do not
won't = will not
isn't = is not
aren't = are not
didn't = did not
hadn't = had not
hasn't = has not
wasn't = was not
shan't = shall not
doesn't = does not
haven't = have not
mustn't = must not
needn't = need not
weren't = were not
couldn't = could not
wouldn't = would not
shouldn't = should not

he's = he is; he has
she's = she is; she has
it's = it is
who's = who is
that's = that is
what's = what is
here's = here is
there's = there is

I'll = I will; I shall
we'll = we will; we shall
he'll = he will; he shall
she'll = she will; she shall
you'll = you will; you shall
who'll = who will; who shall
they'll = they will; they shall

I'd = I had; I would
he'd = he had; he would
we'd = we had; we would
you'd = you had; you would
who'd = who had; who would
they'd = they had; they would

we're = we are
you're = you are
who're = who are
they're = they are

I've = I have
we've = we have
you've = you have
they've = they have

I'm = I am

The apostrophe is also used to show possession, e.g.

The boy's book; girl's coat; man's car; woman's watch.
The boys' books; girls' coats; men's cars; women's watches.

Homophones

These are words that sound alike but have different meanings and spellings.

arc	(curve)	pain	(suffering)	accept	(receive)
ark	(boat; box)	pane	(of glass)	except	(leaving out)
beach	(seashore)	pair	(two)	allowed	(let; permitted)
beech	(tree)	pear	(fruit)	aloud	(loudly)
bean	(plant)	peace	(quiet)	altar	(church table)
been	(past of be)	piece	(a part)	alter	(change)
blew	(blow)	peer	(stare)	dear	(beloved; costly)
blue	(colour)	pier	(jetty)	deer	(animal)
bough	(branch)	place	(position)	flour	(ground wheat)
bow	(bend)	plaice	(fish)	flower	(blossom)
brake	(to stop)	rap	(knock)	foul	(dirty; unfair)
break	(to snap)	wrap	(cover)	fowl	(bird)
chute	(a slide)	sail	(ship)	freeze	(ice; cold)
shoot	(fire)	sale	(selling)	frieze	(wall decoration)
die	(lose life)	slay	(kill)	groan	(moan)
dye	(colour)	sleigh	(sled)	grown	(got bigger)
farther	(further)	stair	(step)	guessed	(did guess)
father	(parent)	stare	(look at)	guest	(visitor)
fort	(castle)	steal	(thieve)	hear	(listen)
fought	(fight)	steel	(metal)	here	(in this place)
hair	(of head)	tail	(end)	heard	(listened)
hare	(animal)	tale	(story)	herd	(of cattle, etc.)
hart	(stag)	pail	(bucket)	hoard	(hidden store)
heart	(of body)	pale	(whitish)	horde	(crowd)
heal	(cure)	scene	(view; place)	hour	(sixty minutes)
heel	(of foot)	seen	(noticed)	our	(belonging to us)
higher	(taller)	tire	(weary)	hole	(hollow place)
hire	(rent)	tyre	(wheel cover)	whole	(all; complete)
hoarse	(husky)	weak	(not strong)	meat	(flesh)
horse	(animal)	week	(seven days)	meet	(come together)
leant	(leaned)	weather	(climate)	meter	(measuring box)
lent	(lend)	whether	(if)	metre	(length measure)
made	(make)	wood	(timber)	moan	(groan)
maid	(girl)	would	(past of will)	mown	(cut grass, etc.)
muscle	(of body)	won	(did win)	signet	(seal, ring)
mussel	(shellfish)	one	(single)	cygnet	(young swan)

knew	(know)	**shore**	(seashore)
new	(just made)	**sure**	(certain)
knight	(Sir)	**their**	(belonging to them)
night	(opp. of day)	**there**	(in that place)
know	(understand)	**they're**	(they are)
no	(not any; opp. of yes)	**theirs**	(belonging to them)
knot	(tied string, etc.)	**there's**	(there is)
not	(no)	**threw**	(throw)
passed	(did pass)	**through**	(from end to end)
past	(time gone by)	**throne**	(king's seat)
ring	(circle; bell sound)	**thrown**	(throw)
wring	(twist)	**board**	(wood; go on ship; lodge)
wait	(stay; serve)	**bored**	(weary; drilled hole)
weight	(Heaviness)	**cereal**	(wheat, oats, etc.)
way	(direction)	**serial**	(in parts)
weigh	(measure heaviness)	**currant**	(fruit)
waste	(not used; useless)	**current**	(flow of water, air, etc.)
waist	(of body)	**cue**	(hint; billiard-stick)
which	(what one? who?)	**queue**	(line of persons, etc.)
witch	(old woman)	**fair**	(just; light; entertainment)
who's	(who is)	**fare**	(price of journey; food)
whose	(belonging to whom?)	**core**	(middle of apple, etc.)
you're	(you are)	**corps**	(group of cadets, etc.)
your	(belonging to you)	**road**	(highway)
it's	(it is)	**rode**	(ride)
its	(belonging to it)	**rowed**	(used oars)
pedal	(foot lever)	**cent**	(coin)
peddle	(to hawk goods)	**sent**	(send)
hall	(room; passage)	**scent**	(smell; perfume)
haul	(pull; amount taken)	**rain**	(water)
him	(he)	**reign**	(rule)
hymn	(song of praise)	**rein**	(strap)
mare	(female horse)	**buy**	(purchase)
mayor	(head of town or city)	**by**	(near to, etc.)
medal	(badge – for bravery, etc.)	**bye**	(a run)
meddle	(interfere)	**to**	(towards)
pray	(ask God)	**too**	(also; more than enough)
prey	(victim; thing hunted)	**two**	(number)

Multiplication Tables

0 × 2 = 0	0 × 3 = 0	0 × 4 = 0	0 × 5 = 0
1 × 2 = 2	1 × 3 = 3	1 × 4 = 4	1 × 5 = 5
2 × 2 = 4	2 × 3 = 6	2 × 4 = 8	2 × 5 = 10
3 × 2 = 6	3 × 3 = 9	3 × 4 = 12	3 × 5 = 15
4 × 2 = 8	4 × 3 = 12	4 × 4 = 16	4 × 5 = 20
5 × 2 = 10	5 × 3 = 15	5 × 4 = 20	5 × 5 = 25
6 × 2 = 12	6 × 3 = 18	6 × 4 = 24	6 × 5 = 30
7 × 2 = 14	7 × 3 = 21	7 × 4 = 28	7 × 5 = 35
8 × 2 = 16	8 × 3 = 24	8 × 4 = 32	8 × 5 = 40
9 × 2 = 18	9 × 3 = 27	9 × 4 = 36	9 × 5 = 45
10 × 2 = 20	10 × 3 = 30	10 × 4 = 40	10 × 5 = 50
11 × 2 = 22	11 × 3 = 33	11 × 4 = 44	11 × 5 = 55
12 × 2 = 24	12 × 3 = 36	12 × 4 = 48	12 × 5 = 60

0 × 6 = 0	0 × 7 = 0	0 × 8 = 0	0 × 9 = 0
1 × 6 = 6	1 × 7 = 7	1 × 8 = 8	1 × 9 = 9
2 × 6 = 12	2 × 7 = 14	2 × 8 = 16	2 × 9 = 18
3 × 6 = 18	3 × 7 = 21	3 × 8 = 24	3 × 9 = 27
4 × 6 = 24	4 × 7 = 28	4 × 8 = 32	4 × 9 = 36
5 × 6 = 30	5 × 7 = 35	5 × 8 = 40	5 × 9 = 45
6 × 6 = 36	6 × 7 = 42	6 × 8 = 48	6 × 9 = 54
7 × 6 = 42	7 × 7 = 49	7 × 8 = 56	7 × 9 = 63
8 × 6 = 48	8 × 7 = 56	8 × 8 = 64	8 × 9 = 72
9 × 6 = 54	9 × 7 = 63	9 × 8 = 72	9 × 9 = 81
10 × 6 = 60	10 × 7 = 70	10 × 8 = 80	10 × 9 = 90
11 × 6 = 66	11 × 7 = 77	11 × 8 = 88	11 × 9 = 99
12 × 6 = 72	12 × 7 = 84	12 × 8 = 96	12 × 9 = 108

0 × 10 = 0	0 × 11 = 0	0 × 12 = 0
1 × 10 = 10	1 × 11 = 11	1 × 12 = 12
2 × 10 = 20	2 × 11 = 22	2 × 12 = 24
3 = 10 = 30	3 × 11 = 33	3 × 12 = 36
4 × 10 = 40	4 × 11 = 44	4 × 12 = 48
5 × 10 = 50	5 × 11 = 55	5 × 12 = 60
6 × 10 = 60	6 × 11 = 66	6 × 12 = 72
7 × 10 = 70	7 × 11 = 77	7 × 12 = 84
8 × 10 = 80	8 × 11 = 88	8 × 12 = 96
9 × 10 = 90	9 × 11 = 99	9 × 12 = 108
10 × 10 = 100	10 × 11 = 110	10 × 12 = 120
11 × 10 = 110	11 × 11 = 121	11 × 12 = 132
12 × 10 = 120	12 × 11 = 132	12 × 12 = 144

Note for Teachers and Parents

Spell It Yourself is based on the belief that there is need for a new type of book which is neither a dictionary nor a conventional spelling book.

Most school children are encouraged to refer to dictionaries for words they wish to use in their written work. But school dictionaries have been compiled, in the first place, for the giving of definitions: the choice of words is usually dictated by children's problems of understanding rather than of spelling. As a result, many everyday words which nevertheless present spelling difficulties are not in school dictionaries, because children are sure to know their meaning.

Some of the commonest spelling errors are made in forming derivatives from root-words which in themselves are quite easy to spell. For example, a child probably knows—or could easily find from a dictionary—how to spell these infinitives: differ, prefer, happen, begin, come, singe, sail, dial, shop, gallop, argue, agree, queue, picnic,,deny, tie, forget, fidget. But there will probably be nothing in the dictionary to help the child to the correct spelling of their present and past participles. How is he or she to know, for example, that the correct forms are 'shopping, shopped', and not 'shoping, shoped'? If the child remembers the doubling of that final consonant, how is he or she to know that the mistake of 'picnicing, picniced' must be corrected by writing 'picnicking, picnicked', and not 'picniccing, picnicced'? Other difficult and irregular word-derivatives not usually in dictionaries include plurals and the comparatives and superlatives of adjectives.

Certain spelling rules may be worked out, but most of these are confused by their many exceptions, and so are of limited usefulness, especially with younger children.

Clearly, children are likely to learn to spell correctly words which they are anxious to use in their own writing. In free writing, children are often not content to mis-spell, if they can avoid it; and they may waste much time, at the expense of the content of their written work, trying to discover the correct spelling of words they need. The usual school spelling-books of groups of words for memorization, children's own word-books, and most junior dictionaries cannot give proper guidance. The teacher often has little time to help with individual problems. It is hoped that this book, *Spell It Yourself*, will provide a useful tool, easy for children to handle for themselves as they need.

Spelling—with the exception of a limited number of the commonest words—seems a subject for individual learning: no two children wish to make use of exactly the same words in their written expression. This reference list, of nearly 8,000 root words, is based upon word-frequency in the upper classes of Junior and Middle Schools; but the list also includes many of the less common words which individual children may need.

In their written compositions children use words whose meanings they understand. They do not often need definitions of the words they cannot spell. Children's ability to read and recognize words is much greater than their ability to spell them; in this book they should be able quickly to find and identify the words they hesitate to spell. The order of the words is alphabetical, and if a child knows the first two letters—as he or she usually does—of the word required, the child can find in the Index the number of the page where he or she should look for it.

The alphabetical basis of the book provides useful training in the use of a dictionary. At the same time, *Spell It Yourself* makes a point of including many words which a school dictionary does not. Word-derivatives are usually shown by suffixes to the right of the columns which need only to be added to the root-words (see the Instructions).

In general, children learn best by finding out for themselves. In this book they will learn to look up words for themselves and to spell them correctly the first time, instead of making mistakes which have later to be corrected. They will steadily increase their written vocabulary, becoming more 'word-conscious' all the time. With this book at their elbow, and under the direction of a teacher aware of its purpose, they will be teaching themselves how to spell.

Index